How To Play
LITTLE LEAGUE
Baseball

By
James Preller

Photos by Richard Hutchings

kidsbooks®
Incorporated

Copyright © 1991 Kidsbooks Inc.
7004 N. California Ave.
Chicago, IL 60645

ISBN 1-56156-010-3

Manufactured in the United States of America

To Maria,
who's always there
for a game of catch.

And to my Mom,
who taught me how.

Acknowledgements

Thanks go out to my team of Baseball Advisors for generously reading the early stages of the manuscript and offering sound advice and insight: Steve Hirdt, President, Larchmont-Mamaroneck (NY) Little League; Don Werner, former Little League official and varsity baseball coach, Westminister School (CT); Frank Waterson, President, Westland Hills (NY) Little League. Also, special thanks to Arthur Marcus, Dennis, Spencer, Steven Josef, Christine, and David for working so hard during the photography sessions for this book. Also, of course, Richard and Amy Hutchings.

CONTENTS

PLAY BALL!

In 1944, when the Little League organization was only five years old, a legendary baseball manager named Connie Mack visited the home of Little League Baseball in Williamsport, Pennsylvania. He watched young players hit and throw. He watched them take infield practice and run the bases. He liked what he saw.

"It would not surprise me one bit," Connie Mack said, "if some of these boys playing Little League Baseball made the major leagues."

And was he ever right! Tom Seaver, Nolan Ryan, Tony Gwynn, Will Clark, Wade Boggs, Bret Saberhagen, Dwight Gooden, Orel Hershiser—these are just a few of the former Little Leaguers who have gone on to greatness in the major leagues.

But back in 1944 Connie Mack didn't know something we know today. Girls didn't play Little League Baseball back then; they didn't join until 1974. Or else Connie Mack might have said that it was only a matter of time before some of today's boys— and, yes, girls—make it to the pros.

Of course, not many players can throw a ball 100 miles an hour like Nolan Ryan or hit a ball 500 feet like Darryl Strawberry. Only a select few of today's Little Leaguers will make it to the pros.

But whether you dream of becoming a Hall-of-Famer, or if you simply want to play a little better, then you should have the exact same goal. You want to be able to say, "I did my best...and I had fun."

A Wonderful Game

Are you ready? Here's something that might surprise you: *If you read this book you will NOT become a better ballplayer*.

You can't just *read* about a sport to improve. You've got to go out and put your new knowledge to work. You've got to practice.

By reading this book, though, you *are* on the right path to becoming a better ballplayer. No matter what your skills are now—whether you've just joined your first Little League team or if you have a few years experience under your belt—I promise you'll learn something from this book that you can take out on the field with you. You *can* become a better ballplayer. All you have to do is try.

Most players and coaches agree that if baseball is played well, it is more enjoyable. But playing well doesn't only mean hitting home runs and pitching no-hitters. It means playing fair. It means playing as a team, trying your best, and always remembering that you're out there to have a good time.

Take a moment to remember what an umpire does just before the game begins. He yells, "Play ball!" Think about it: *Play*...ball. He doesn't say, "Okay everybody, go out and have a rotten time!" He doesn't scream, "*Work* ball!" He says "Play ball!" to remind everyone that baseball is a game to be enjoyed.

Little League Baseball is a game that can teach you there are more important things in life than just competition—like honesty, friendship, and fairness. That's the real meaning of Little League Baseball—learning how to try hard and play your best. Learning how to win...and how to lose. Learning how to be a good sport, even when things don't go your way.

Strive to become the best player you can be. Practice and improve your skills. Run your fastest and swing your mightiest. Even dare to dream about becoming a pro. But always remember the call of the umpire, remember the cry that echoes across ball fields from California to Maine: "PLAY BALL!"

And then go out there, rub a little dirt in your hands, and have the time of your life.

A Word to the Wise

Throughout this book I'll describe the conventional, or "classic," methods of catching, hitting, pitching, running, and fielding. These are proven methods that have worked for thousands of players around the world.

There is no single, standard way of playing—everyone has his or her own style. But remember, there are hundreds of variations you can use. Your own comfort is what's most important. Still, I encourage you to learn the classic way and *then* make the adjustments that help you feel most comfortable. A relaxed player is a confident player. And a confident player is a successful player. Learn the techniques that have worked for others. Then— as long as it's successful—do your own thing.

CATCHING AND THROWING THE BASEBALL

Players can't improve very much until they master the basics, or *fundamentals*, of the game. Just as a builder must first make a strong foundation before he can construct a building, a ballplayer must develop solid fundamentals before he or she can become an outstanding player.

That means learning how to throw accurately and catch the ball consistently. If you can do that—*and you can*—then you'll help your team win some ballgames.

Before you have a catch, make sure that you're warmed up. Take a short jog and do a few simple stretching exercises to get your body loose and limber. Always begin a catch by standing just a short distance from your teammate. As the muscles in your arm loosen up, gradually increase the distance. (To learn more about sports fitness, go to the library and seek out the excellent book, *Play Ball! The Official Little League Fitness Guide* by Frank W. Jobe, M.D., and Diane R. Moynes, M.S., R.P.T.)

Grip the Ball Correctly

For an accurate, consistent throw, you should grip the ball the same way every time. The correct grip for fielders is the same grip a pitcher uses for a fastball. Place your forefinger and middle finger over the top of the ball, resting on the stitches, or "seams."

THE CLASSIC GRIP: Two fingers across the seams over the top of the ball and the thumb underneath.

DON'T JAM THE BALL AGAINST YOUR PALM: There should be some air between the ball and your palm.

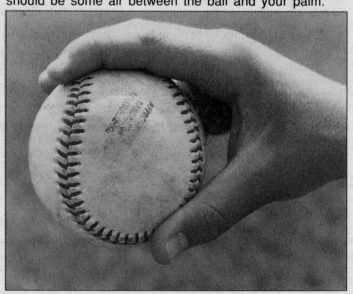

Your thumb goes underneath, also on a seam. You don't really use your remaining fingers at all; hold them curled slightly to the side of the ball. By holding the ball on the seams, you'll naturally put a backward rotation on the ball. This backspin will give your throw greater accuracy.

Ready, Aim, Throw

Although you throw in one motion, it's helpful to understand the various stages of a successful throw.

Let's begin with your stance. You should be balanced, with your knees slightly bent and your feet spread about twelve inches apart. Your eyes should be on the target at all times. Aim at the target by pretending that you have an extra pair of eyes on the side of your non-throwing shoulder and hip (if you're a righty, that's your left side; if you're a lefty, that's your right side). Now turn to the side and "look" at the target with your extra set of eyes.

Start with the ball already in your glove. Bring your hands together near your belt. Get a firm, proper grip on the ball. Bring the ball back behind your body, keeping your elbow slightly bent. Most of your weight should be on your back leg. While still aiming with your shoulder, step toward the target. Bring your back elbow up over your shoulder as you continue making a circle with your throwing arm. Notice that your weight has shifted to your front foot.

When you release the ball, whip your wrist forward in a strong, snapping motion for extra power. Follow through by bending forward and letting your arm come all the way across the front of your body. Hey, not bad—a perfect, chest-high throw!

The Skip and Step

To get even more power on your throw, use the skip-and-step method. It's also called the "crow hop." Start by aiming your

CATCHING AND
THROWING ARE
THE BASICS OF
BASEBALL: You
don't need to be
a superstar to
help your team.

8

shoulder at the target and holding your hands together at the waist. Lift your front foot off the ground and take a small hop, or *skip*, on your back foot. Complete your throw by pushing off your back foot and stepping toward the target. Practice this motion whenever you have a catch—it will give you extra momentum for an extra-strong throw.

Points to Remember

- Use the same grip every time.
- Aim with your non-throwing shoulder.
- Take a short skip-and-step for extra momentum.
- Make sure your elbow rises above your shoulder when you throw.
- Put your whole body into it—follow through by bending your back and bringing your arm down across your body.

Catching the Ball

To catch the ball, you should be in a relaxed position, with your feet spread out for balance and mobility. Remember, bend your knees. (Baseball is a game played with bent knees—hitting, catching, throwing, it doesn't matter! Keep those knees bent and your weight on the balls of your feet.) Hold your arms out in front of your body, with your elbows bent. Make a good target with your open glove at about chest level. Perfect, now you're ready.

The position in which you hold the glove depends upon where the ball is thrown. If the ball is above your waist, hold the glove with your fingers pointing up. If the ball is below your waist, turn your fingers down.

The best fielders have what are called "soft hands." It doesn't mean their hands are actually *soft*. Players have soft hands when they "give" a little upon impact. That is, your hands and arms

9

FINGERS POINT UP when catching a ball above your waist.

FINGERS POINT DOWN when catching a ball below your waist.

move in toward your body as you catch the ball. This absorbs the force of the throw and helps you control the ball.

Think of catching a ball as if someone were handing you a birthday present. You gently *receive* it; you never grab it like a spoiled child. The same is true for a ball. Let it come to you—don't stab or swipe at it. Remember: soft hands.

Follow the ball with your eyes all the way into the glove. Most errors are made when players get lazy and take their eyes off the ball. As the pros say, "Watch the ball into your glove."

Lastly, catch the ball with two hands. Yes, I know, you only have one glove. Use your throwing hand to cover the ball once it reaches your glove. And give the ball a good squeeze with your glove. You'll keep a lot of balls from popping out that way.

Points to Remember:

- You should be in a state of "relaxed readiness"—arms extended, elbows bent, legs spread out and balanced on the balls of your feet.
- Don't stab or swipe at the ball; let it come to you.
- Absorb the force of the throw by "giving" with your elbows.
- Watch the ball into your glove.
- Cover the ball with your throwing hand once you've made the catch.

Taking Care of Your Glove

Most professional ballplayers have owned their gloves for years. They know how important it is to have a good, reliable glove—so they take care of it. So should you.

It's especially important to condition, or "break in," a new glove. Go to a sports store and purchase some glove or leather

11

oil. At night, carefully rub the oil into your glove. This will soften and strengthen the leather, making your glove more flexible. Be sure to wipe away all the excess oil once you've finished. Now, place two hardballs, or one large softball, into the center of the glove. Tie the glove closed with a piece of string. Leave it tied overnight. This will help create a natural "pocket"—so the ball will be much less likely to pop out when you try to catch it.

HITTING

There you are at the plate, bat in hand, looking out at a tough pitcher with a nasty fastball. He rubs the ball with his hands and gets the signal from the catcher. More than anything, he wants you to fail. And, even if you are very, very good, you probably will.

Think about it: If you get a hit only once out of three times up, that's a .333 average. Most Major League players would love to hit that well. But let's just say you're talented enough to hit .333—that also means you'll fail two out of every three times you come to the plate. Maybe that's why so many people believe that hitting a baseball is the hardest thing to do in any sport.

If you ever go through a time when you are struggling as a hitter, remember this: Babe Ruth, perhaps the greatest hitter of all time, struck out 1,360 times! In baseball, everyone fails at one time or another. Everyone makes mistakes. But the best players never give up. That's why no one remembers all the times Babe Ruth struck out. They remember the home runs—all 714 of them!

Just You and the Ball

Hitting can be the loneliest part of the game. When it's your turn to bat, none of your teammates can help. It's just you, the pitcher, and the ball. And after the pitcher releases the pitch, it's just you and the ball. Sound tough? It is, but hitting can also be a lot of fun. (And the better you hit, the more fun it is!)

Smash—it's a great feeling when the ball connects with the sweet spot of the bat and rockets into the outfield. Your hit sets off a flurry of activity. The ball bounces into the gap between left and center. Suddenly outfielders are racing across the grass. Infielders are covering bases or coming out for the relay throw. Runners are tearing around the basepaths and the third-base coach is windmilling his arms, waving a runner home. The on-deck batter moves a few feet behind the plate; with his palms downward, he's signaling "Slide!" The catcher grabs the ball on a bounce, the runner slides, a cloud of dust rises in the air, and all eyes turn toward the umpire...

"Safe!"

Standing on second base with a double, you've just helped your team win a big game. All because you've learned how to hit. You've practiced. And you've practiced the right way.

Okay, let's start talking about the basics of hitting. It doesn't start with which bat you use. It doesn't start with what kind of stance you prefer. Instead, as the doctor said, *it's all in your head.*

Start With Positive Thinking

Good hitters all have something in common. They all have a positive mental approach. They *want* to hit. They believe in themselves. When they go up to the plate, they are concentrated on the task before them. All of their attention is focused on the pitcher and the ball—they aren't daydreaming or looking to their friends in the stands.

You can help yourself as a hitter by *thinking* like a hitter. Spend time reviewing in your mind all the things it takes to hit the ball

THUMBS UP: It's a great feeling when you come up with a big hit to help your team.

well. It helps if you create a positive *image* in your mind. Picture yourself hitting a hard line drive into the outfield. See all the details: Imagine the pitcher starting the windup. Imagine standing at the plate in your stance. You are confident and concentrated. See yourself stride forward, take a swing, and connect with the ball. There—it's easy!

Hitting is concentration. The best time for you to prepare to hit is when you are on-deck, just before you're about to hit. Begin by studying the pitcher. Does she throw a good fastball? Then you'll need to be a little quicker with your swing. Is the pitcher wild? Remind yourself not to swing at balls out of the strike zone. Free your mind of distractions. Follow the ball during the entire windup. Locate the exact point where the pitcher releases the ball. Time your practice swings with the pitcher, pretending that you are already in the batter's box.

15

Use your time on-deck to review the fundamentals of hitting. Tell yourself to watch the ball all the way. Your goal is to actually see the bat hit the ball. Keep your head down, stride forward, take a level swing.

The best hitters *want* to hit. They're ready and eager. Somehow, they just *know* they can hit the ball. They also know that if they doubt themselves, they won't be successful. There's no place for negative thinking in the batter's box. Tell yourself, "I'm a hitter. I'm going to get a hit." This is the power of positive thinking—and it works!

Points to Remember:

- Prepare yourself mentally before each turn at the plate—concentrate on what you have to do to succeed.

HITTING *IS* CONCENTRATION: The best hitters take their time on-deck seriously. They mentally prepare themselves for their turn at bat.

- Study the pitcher closely.
- Make an image in your mind of how it looks when you hit the ball well.
- Use positive thinking—tell yourself, "I know I can get a hit."
- Remind yourself of the basics: Get a good pitch to hit, keep your head down, stride toward the ball.

Keep Your Eye on the Ball

There are three important things to know about hitting—*watch the ball, watch the ball, watch the ball!*

Yes, hitting can be a lot more complicated than just watching the ball. You've got to know the strike zone. You've got to get a good pitch to hit. You've got to develop a quick, accurate swing. You've got to keep your hands up and stride correctly. You've got to shift your weight and turn your hips at the right moment. You've got to get good arm extension and keep your shoulders fairly level.

Yes, there are a thousand things you can think about—and each one can mess you up if you think about it too much. Each one won't help you a bit unless you *keep your eye on the ball.*

Get a Good Pitch to Hit

Most batters have a "happy zone," or a place they particularly like to see the ball. Some batters are low ball hitters. Others like pitches that are inside. Some prefer pitches out over the plate. As you play, you might find that you hit particularly well against certain types of pitches. Make a mental note of this. Tell yourself, "I seem to hit low balls well. Next time a low ball comes in, I'm going to be sure to get a good cut at it."

17

When you do that, you've taken a key step in your development as a hitter. You are, as the pros so often say, "looking for your pitch."

The opposite is also true. If high pitches give you trouble, then lay off them. Take a strike if you have to—after all, the rules give you three. And it only takes one swing to get a hit.

Know the Strike Zone

The strike zone is as wide as home plate, exactly seventeen inches. Vertically, it extends from your knees to about your armpits. To become a smart hitter, you must know your strike zone. Hitting is hard enough without swinging at pitches you can't even reach.

While you're at bat somebody may call out to you: "A walk's as good as a hit!" Well, guess what. They're right. The only way to measure the quality of a team's offense is by how many runs that team scores. But you shouldn't feel like you have to hit a home run to help your team score runs. If a wild pitcher is offering you a free pass to first base, then take it. Sometimes a walk may be all it takes to rattle a pitcher...or start a big rally.

> QUICK TIP: In baseball, it's often the ordinary things done well that win games.

A smart pitcher might see if she can tempt you to swing at a bad pitch. She'll throw a pitch a little bit outside. Do you swing? If so, she'll keep throwing you balls—and keep getting you out. Because even the best hitters turn into bad hitters when they swing at bad pitches. If you're an intelligent hitter, you won't swing at a pitch that's out of the strike zone. You'll have discipline. You'll make the pitcher throw strikes.

Maybe you'll even get your favorite pitch to hit. Then, watch out. Base hit—you've just smoked a line drive into center field!

Points to Remember

- Watch the ball, watch the ball, watch the ball!
- Look for a good pitch to hit.
- Know the strike zone—don't swing at bad pitches.
- Remember, a walk is truly as good as a hit.

Choose the Bat That's Right for You

Which is the right bat for you? The one with all the hits in it, of course!

When selecting a bat, there are a few things to consider. Don't be fooled into thinking you need a heavy bat to hit the ball a long way. Remember, the speed of your swing is more important than the weight of your bat. A heavy bat that you can't control won't help you. Gone are the days when Babe Ruth swaggered to the plate carrying a big 40-ounce piece of lumber; modern ballplayers usually swing shorter, lighter bats that weigh 31-34 ounces. Mickey Mantle, Ted Williams, and Willie Mays all used light bats. Each one hit more than 500 career home runs. They knew that the speed of a quick swing was a prime source of their power.

What's more, a light bat is easier to control—and that means you'll have a more consistent swing and a higher batting average.

A Loose, Relaxed Grip

Some Little Leaguers hold a bat as if they were trying to squeeze it to death! You can see them, tense and nervous,

IS THIS BAT TOO HEAVY? Here's an easy way to find out. Grip the end of the bat and hold it straight out for ten seconds. If your arm gets tired and shaky after a few seconds, then you should try a lighter bat.

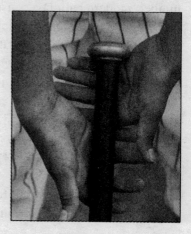

LAY THE BAT IN YOUR FINGERS. Then slowly wrap your hands around the bat. There—that's a good grip— strong, but not too tight.

their knuckles white with anxiety. That's not good. When you are hitting, you should try to be calm and relaxed. Your muscles need to be fluid, like water, ready to move in an instant. When you hold a bat too tightly, your whole body stiffens and it restricts your swing.

Grip the bat toward the bottom, near the knob, with your hands together. If you are in your stance, then your back hand is at the top; the hand that's nearest the pitcher should be on the bottom.

Some players like to choke up on the bat. This can help you swing faster and give you better bat control. Power hitters tend to hold the bat near the end, at the knob. This gives them maximum arm leverage for more power. Try it both ways. See what feels best for you. Even if you like to hold the bat at the end, you may want to choke up when there are two strikes on you.

Points to Remember

- ◆ Stay loose.
- ◆ Grip the bat firmly, but not *too* tight.
- ◆ Keep your hands together.
- ◆ Choke up for better control; hold the bat at the bottom for better power.

The Stance

There are as many different types of stances as there are different ballplayers. Some players crouch real low, others stand fairly straight. Some have closed stances, others prefer open stances. Some hold their bat straight up, while others hold their bats parallel to the ground. There is no single correct way. As long as you get hits, you must be doing

21

HIT THE BALL WITH THE "SWEET SPOT" OF THE BAT. The most solid hits occur when the bat meets the ball in the area indicated here.

CHOKING UP CAN GIVE YOU MORE BAT CONTROL AND A QUICKER SWING. With two strikes on you, choke up and try hitting the ball back up the middle.

CHECK TO MAKE SURE YOUR BAT "COVERS" the entire plate area. You have to be able to reach the ball if you want to hit it.

something right. The important thing is that you feel comfortable and you don't do anything that keeps you from playing your best.

That said, there are aspects of the conventional batting stance which you may find helpful.

To begin with, you must be able to reach—and hit—any pitch that could be called a strike. A quick check is to bend slightly and touch the far end of the plate with your bat. Be careful not to stand too close to the plate, where it would be difficult to hit the ball with the meatiest part of your bat.

A Question of Balance

Your feet should be parallel to each other, at shoulders' width. Bend at the hip a little; then bend at your knees. Can you feel that? Your weight has shifted to the balls of your feet. This provides you with a solid base to hit from—a strong foundation. Many batters get into the terrible habit of "swinging from their heels." Their weight carries them *away* from the plate. This pulls their head away and takes their eye off the ball. That's no way to hit. They lack the strong foundation—*the balance*—a player needs in order to have a good approach to the ball.

You should hold your hands even with your chest, approximately four to eight inches from your back armpit. Your front arm should be parallel to the ground. Your front elbow should be at the same level as your hands. The back elbow can be a bit higher. With the bat held this way, you'll have the freedom of movement for a quick, powerful swing.

Make sure that both eyes have a clear view of the pitcher. Hold your head up straight. A good, clear view of the ball can't be stressed enough.

By the way, statues are nice—but they don't belong in the batter's box. When you are in your stance you should be loose. To accomplish this, take a few practice swings before you step into the box. Once you're set, try rocking gently, or swaying your bat a little. To be quick with the bat, your body and hands must be relaxed. Then, quiet down as the pitcher begins the windup.

Points to Remember

- Your body is relaxed and balanced—don't be a statue.
- Your feet are directly under your shoulders, about twelve inches apart.

- Your hands are even with your chest about four to eight inches from your back armpit.
- Your front arm is parallel to the ground.
- Your eyes have a clear view of the pitcher.
- Your weight is mostly on the back foot.
- You are bent at the hip and at the knees.

The Starter Mechanism

Think about how many things in sports go backward before they go forward.

A golfer brings the club back, then swings it forward. A tennis player gently brings back the racket, then swings it forward. A pitcher in a windup rocks back, then strides forward. In each case it helps the player get consistency and power. The same is true in hitting.

As the pitcher begins, so do you. The pitcher rocks back into the windup; you shift your weight back. In the same motion you also move your hands up and back to the hitting position, close to your back shoulder. Some players even like to cock their front hip and shoulder in toward the plate. It's a small, subtle motion, like pulling a door back before slamming it shut. There, you've pressed the starter mechanism—now you've gained extra momentum to spring forward, bringing all your muscles into action as you swing.

The Stride

The stride is a key timing aspect of your swing. But remember, you don't stride and swing at the same time. *First* you stride, *then* you swing.

The stride is a simple, gentle motion. In fact, you actually keep your weight and hands back when you stride forward. Think of your stride as if you were stepping on an egg and you didn't want to break it. You only take a short step, about six to eight inches. If you step too far, it's called overstriding or lunging. Overstriding will throw off your balance. It also creates too much body motion, making it impossible for you to keep your head still. And you've got to keep your head still if you want to see properly. If you don't believe it, try reading this page while jumping up and down!

Forward and Toward

We've come to another critical point in your hitting: *You must stride forward, toward the pitcher*. Many players have a tendency to stride away from the plate. This is called "stepping into the bucket." When a hitter steps into the bucket it creates all sorts of problems. The hips open too soon. The head, which is attached to the body, must follow; it becomes impossible to keep your eyes on the ball. The inside shoulder, facing the pitcher, follows the front foot and flies open too soon—pulling you off balance and causing you to lose most of your power.

That's why you must stride *forward and toward*.

When you stride forward, your hips remain closed, or square, parallel to the plate. Your shoulders are level. Your head is down, focused on the pitcher's throwing hand. All of your attention is concentrated on the ball. You are about to bring your weight forward; you are about to begin your swing. You are perfectly balanced, ready for any pitch, high or low, inside or outside. You are coiled like a snake, ready to strike.

Points to Remember

- Stride first, swing second.
- Stride softly, but carry a big stick—you only need to stride a few inches.

- Stride forward and toward.
- Keep hips and shoulders aligned, parallel to the plate.
- Keep your head still; don't pull away from the ball.

The Swing

By now you've made your big decision. You've decided to swing. Suddenly a lot of things happen all at once—your hands, arms, legs, shoulders, hips, and feet are all in motion. Let's look at what should be happening one thing at a time.

You've made your stride and planted your front foot on the ground. Now your weight begins to shift from back leg to front. Importantly, your entire body begins a sudden, powerful rotation. As your hands, arms, and bat come forward through the strike zone, your hips and shoulders quickly turn to face the pitcher. Your back leg pushes your weight forward and bends at the knee, forming an L. Your back foot pivots and points directly at the pitcher. All the while, your head is down, still focused on the ball.

The Movement of the Bat

Any mathematician can tell you that the fastest way to get from point A to point B is with a straight line. The same is true for your swing. You want to bring your bat from the hitting position (point A) to the ball (point B) in the quickest way possible. Your success as a hitter depends upon the speed and accuracy of your swing.

The ideal is a short, quick, compact swing. As you get older, and pitchers get faster, a quick bat will become even more important.

Points to Remember

- Your weight shifts from back leg to front leg.
- The back foot pivots and faces the pitcher.

27

THE STANCE: The batter has a balanced, solid foundation.

THE STRIDE: The batter rocks back gently; the hands go back. The batter strides forward and toward. The weight and hands are still back.

THE SWING: The hands move quickly through the plate area. Head is still down. Hips and shoulders swing open.

CONTACT: Weight comes fully forward to the front leg. Head is still down. Wrists begin turning over.

THE FOLLOW THROUGH: Bat comes around in a wide arc.

- ◆ Your hips and shoulders pivot together and face the pitcher.
- ◆ A short, quick swing is best—avoid excess motion.

Contact!

The impact of a bat and ball lasts less than 1/100th of a second. But what a feeling!

At contact, the palm of your top hand faces the sky. This hand provides most of the arm power to your swing. The bottom hand's palm faces the ground—this hand guides the bat and supplies extra power.

Your belt buckle should be facing the pitcher. Your back leg has formed an L. All of your weight has shifted to your front leg, which is firmly planted on the ground.

29

One way to improve the speed and accuracy of your swing, thus hitting the ball with greater authority, is to practice throwing your hands at the ball. Of course, you can't exactly "throw your hands"—they're attached to your arms. Instead, imagine throwing your hands by quickly snapping your wrists at the ball. Your elbows and wrists extend to create a whipping motion that generates speed.

Points to Remember

- ◆ Your top hand generates power; your bottom hand guides the bat.
- ◆ Your eye should be on the barrel of the bat—you actually try to see the bat hit the ball.
- ◆ Throw your hands at the ball—let your wrists snap to create a whipping motion.
- ◆ Your shoulders, hips, and head are aligned and working together.

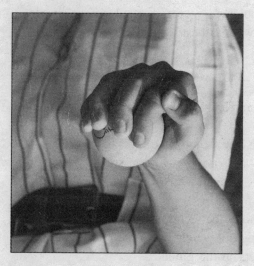

YOU CAN WORK TO STRENGTHEN YOUR WRISTS by squeezing a small rubber ball.

Follow Through

A good follow through is essential in every sport—basketball, tennis, golf, football, and yes, baseball. It provides you with power and consistency. Imagine what would happen if you didn't follow through. During practice, try stopping the bat at the point of contact. The ball doesn't go very far, does it?

Your swing should be one smooth motion, from beginning to end. You are swinging "through" the ball, rather than "at" it. The bat moves in a sweeping arc from shoulder to shoulder. At contact, your top hand "rolls over" your bottom hand. This is where strong wrists really help.

After the bat comes around to the back of your shoulders, try to regain your balance quickly. Because if you've hit the ball, you're not a batter anymore. Now you're a runner...and every second counts.

A Level Swing

What's the best hit—a grounder, a fly, or a line drive? It depends on what kind of hitter you are. Fly balls can be great...if you're strong enough to hit the ball a long way; but if you don't have that kind of power, your fly will only become an easy out. You'd be better off hitting hard grounders.

A fly ball is a fairly routine play. It only takes one fielder on the other team to catch it. Grounders, on the other hand, demand a lot more activity. An infielder must first catch the grounder, then make a strong throw, and then the first baseman must catch it! That's a lot more work—and lot more opportunity for mistakes—than on a fly. But the best hit of all is a solid line drive. Research *shows that more line drives result in basehits than any other kind of hit*. And the way to hit line drives is with a hard, quick, *level* swing.

Don't Try to "Murder" the Ball

One of the ugliest sights in baseball is watching a good hitter strike out because he was trying to "murder" the ball. This attitude only ruins the hitter's swing by creating a lot of bad habits. Yes, as a hitter you should swing hard. But that doesn't mean you should go for the fences with every cut. As a hitter, you must make contact with the ball for good things to happen.

Many of baseball's best hitters are able to hit to all fields. In other words, they hit the ball where it's pitched. To hit like this takes patience, practice, and intelligence. Smart hitters know that it's impossible to pull an outside pitch. They realize that if they "go with the pitch," they'll have much better results.

If the ball is on the outside part of the plate, you should step in and drill the ball to the opposite field. If the pitch is inside, get your bat out early, turn on the ball with your hips and shoulders, and pull it down the line. If the pitch is right down the middle, then stroke it right back at the pitcher.

Flaws and Corrections

Below you'll find a description of a few common mistakes that even the best hitters sometimes make. You'll also find suggestions for how to correct them.

Trouble with High Pitches

You may be swinging under the ball because your hands are too low. Try holding your hands a little higher.

Weakly Hit Balls

Your loss of power is probably because you aren't swinging hard enough or because you have a poor follow-through. To correct this, work on strengthening your wrists, hands, and fingers. Squeeze a rubber ball every day. Remind yourself to swing "through the ball"—not "at" it.

Uppercutting the Ball

This happens when you fail to keep your shoulders level. When you uppercut, your back shoulder "collapses" and your front shoulder rises too high. You can solve this by raising your back elbow a little more than usual. Also, lower your front shoulder a bit and aim it at the pitcher.

Overstriding

You lose power and control because you stride too far or too heavily. This also makes it hard to keep your head still. Spend time working on your stride. Draw a line about six to eight inches from your front foot and make sure that you don't cross it. Also, step lightly—pretend you are stepping on an egg that you don't want to break.

Stepping into the Bucket

Keep your weight on the balls of your feet. You can do this by bending at your waist, and then bending at your knees. Importantly, train yourself to stride directly forward, toward the pitcher. You may also try closing your stance a little.

Fear of the Ball

Fear of the ball is a natural reaction—after all, a baseball isn't exactly soft! But you've got to overcome this fear to be successful. First, you should know that not many injuries occur from a pitched ball. Yes, it can sting, but the feeling quickly passes. Here are two things you can try: 1) Practice hitting with a tennis ball. Then, have a friend soft toss a hardball to you. Gradually work your way up to full speed; 2) Have a coach pitch inside to you and practice getting out of the way. Once you realize you can avoid tight pitches, you'll be less afraid of them.

A Batting Slump

Maybe you can't find one specific reason why you aren't hitting. But somehow, nothing feels quite right. This is a time for you to review the basics. Put in extra practice with a hitting tee. One way to get back in the groove is to try hitting the ball directly back to the pitcher. Don't try to murder the ball, just make contact. Remember, be patient and don't lose your confidence. Keep the faith—those line drives will come again!

A Word About Practice

Everybody says, "You've got to *practice* to become a better player." It must get pretty boring to hear after a while. But that doesn't mean it isn't true.

To get the most out of practice, it's helpful to understand what it is you accomplish by practicing.

Essentially, you are establishing *habits*. Good habits, hopefully, or else it's not good practice. Wade Boggs once said,"Practice

HITTING FROM A TEE may be the single most effective way to work on and improve your swing.

doesn't make perfect. Perfect practice makes perfect." What Boggs meant is that practicing doesn't help if you don't go about things properly. When you practice, you should try to do things the right way, *every time*. That's how you develop good habits.

Drill #1—Perfect to a "T"

A lot of young players think that hitting from a tee is only for beginners. And they're dead wrong. Many pros still use hitting tees as part of their game—just ask Don Mattingly!

Hitting from a tee may be the most effective way for you to improve your swing. With a tee, you don't need to worry about the pitcher, the score, or any other details of the game. The tee gives you the chance to work on all the little things that contribute to a good swing. For example, you can work on details such as the speed of your swing, your approach to the ball, or your follow through.

Here are a few techniques you can practice while hitting from a tee:

- ◆ KEEP YOUR STRIDE CONSISTENT every time you swing. Watch where your front foot lands. Make sure you step toward the imaginary pitcher.
- ◆ PRACTICE KEEPING YOUR HEAD DOWN and focused on the tee—even after contact.
- ◆ MAKE SURE YOUR BACK ELBOW DOESN'T DIP before you swing—that could cause an uppercut that will hurt your batting average.
- ◆ SNAP YOUR WRISTS and "roll them over" with every swing. Swing "through" the ball, not "at" it.
- ◆ BE SURE TO STAY BALANCED THROUGHOUT YOUR SWING. If you seem off balance, that probably means you are overswinging. Make an adjustment. Step into the pitch and try to hit the ball up the middle.

- ◆ ASK SOMEONE WHO KNOWS ABOUT HITTING TO OBSERVE while you practice. A "second eye" may help you correct a flaw in your swing.

QUICK TIP: Remember, set up the tee a few inches in front of the plate. In a game, you actually hit the ball *before* it reaches the plate.

Drill #2—Swing Those Hips!

Here's a simple drill that will help you experience what it feels like to properly turn your hips on the ball. Remember, a strong hip turn helps you get your whole body into the swing—and that's how you generate power.

First, hold a bat at both ends behind your waist, parallel to the ground. Take your normal batting stance. Imagine that the ball is on its way. Stride forward and then, after you plant your front foot, use the bat to help turn your hips toward the ball. Your shoulders and hips turn together, as if you were an old door slamming shut. Your belt buckle should be facing the imaginary pitcher when you complete your swing.

Practice this drill until it becomes automatic for you to turn on the ball with power.

BUNTING

Bunting has almost become a lost art. Due to modern baseball's love affair with the long ball, combined with the popularity of artificial turf, you see fewer and fewer good bunts each year. It's too bad, because a perfect bunt is a masterpiece. It is the triumph of speed over strength, skill over dumb luck. The bunt is a potent offensive weapon that often raises batting averages, builds runs, and wins games.

Players bunt for one of two reasons: to get a hit or to advance a runner. When you bunt to advance a runner it is called a sacrifice bunt. This is because the batter is "sacrificing" his chance of getting a hit for the benefit of the team. His job is to move the runner farther around the bases, even if it means he'll be thrown out at first.

The Sacrifice Bunt

It's late in the game and the score is tied, 0-0. Both teams are locked in a pitcher's duel, with hits few and far between. But now there's hope; the lead-off batter reaches first on an error. There's no one out...and it's your turn at the plate. You look down to your coach and he flashes you the bunt sign. If you can advance the runner to second, it will only take a single to score the go-ahead run. The question is, what do you do now?

The Square-around Method

Take your normal batting stance. As the pitcher goes into his windup, turn your body to face the pitcher by swinging your back foot around, parallel to your front foot (the toes of both feet point to the pitcher). Slide your top hand about twelve inches up the bat and hold the bat firmly in front of the plate. Keep your arms relaxed and your elbows bent, in front of your body. The bat should be parallel to the ground, at about chest level. Bend at the waist, bend at the knees; your weight should be forward, on the balls of your feet. Now you're set.

Bunt only at strikes. If the pitch looks like a ball, pull the bat away. Since you are holding the bat at chest level, it's already at the top of the strike zone. If the ball is above your bat, then you know it's not a strike.

Catch the Ball With the Bat

Bunted balls should drop down to the ground soon after hitting the bat. You achieve this by hitting the top half of the ball. Your bunt should be in a place that's difficult for any fielder to reach. Don't bunt the ball directly to the pitcher. It's generally best to guide the ball so that it rolls along either baseline. That's why you don't swing at the ball, or even push at it. Instead, it's almost as if you are trying to catch the ball with your bat. You aim by holding the bat at a slight angle.

QUICK TIP: To help "deaden" the ball, pull the bat back slightly upon contact. Now it won't come off the bat too hard.

HOLD THE BAT IN FRONT OF THE PLATE. You'll have a much better chance of hitting the ball into fair territory.

If the pitch is down by your knees, go after the ball by lowering your entire body. After you've hit the ball, and only after you've hit the ball, quickly run to first. But don't try to run and hit at the same time. As long as you advance the runner, you'll have helped your team build a run.

The Pivot Method

The pivot method isn't much different from the square-around method. The only real difference is in your footwork. Instead of sliding your back foot forward, you simply pivot on both feet. The advantage of the pivot method is that it's quicker than squaring around, so you can wait a few more seconds before getting into bunting position. This way you won't tip off your intentions to the opposing team.

THE SQUARE-AROUND METHOD: Make sure you don't step out of the batter's box or on home plate. In either case, you'll be automatically out if you hit the ball.

THE PIVOT METHOD: Pivot both feet so your toes face the pitcher. Note: in this photo, the batter should probably be bending more, lower to the ground.

Bunting for a Hit

If you are a struggling hitter, or if you'd just like one more trick up your sleeve, you should practice bunting for a hit. One of the keys to bunting for a hit is picking the right situation. If you are leading off an inning, a bunt basehit just might be the thing to ignite your offense. On the other hand, if you are the team's slugger...and the bases are loaded...then it's not time to bunt. Swing away and try to drive those runners home.

When's the best time to bunt for a hit? Well, when no one expects it. Study the defense. Does the third baseman have a weak arm? Is she back on her heels...or perhaps playing too deep? Then lay one down the third-base line. Does the pitcher fall off to one side after each pitch? Then you may want to bunt it to the other side of the mound. Is the grass wet and slippery? Then shake things up. Drop down a bunt and run like the wind. If you are up against a particularly tough pitcher, a bunt might be your best chance for a hit. Go for it. Just remember, your best chance is when you catch the other team by surprise.

Practice making the pivot quickly by turning and dropping the bat down at the last moment. As you improve, you can work with your coach on even more complex forms of bunting such as fake bunts and drag bunts and push bunts.

Points to Remember

- Keep your arms relaxed and hold the bat in front of your body.
- Hold the bat at about chest level, parallel to the ground.
- Avoid popping up—bunt the top half of the ball.
- Deaden the ball by pulling the bat back slightly upon contact.
- Study the defense. Bunt to their weak spot.

DRILL #3—Glove Bunting

Here's a simple exercise that will give you the hang of "catching" the ball with your bat. Step into the batting box wearing a glove. Pivot and take your normal bunting stance. Now, catch the pitch with your glove hand. There's one trick, though—you can only move your glove up and down, or from side to side. Be sure to hold your body the same way as if you were bunting. After a while, try it with a bat. Chances are, you'll have improved in minutes!

DRILL #4—Target Practice

Since the placement of the bunted ball is so important, you should work on guiding the ball to key locations. Begin by placing a bat or a spare shin guard about ten feet away, along each baseline. Bunt the ball five times down each line trying to hit the targets. Take turns batting with a few teammates. Keep track of how many times you hit the target. You'll not only improve the location of your bunts, you'll have fun too!

RUNNING THE BASES

There's a lot more to baserunning than merely running fast. Sure, speed helps, but good judgment and a knowledge of the game are often more important.

A good baserunner always knows the score, the number of outs, and where the ball is located. Before the game, every player should study the field condition. Is the outfield grass wet and slippery? If so, you might be able to take an extra base. At the least, you'll be alert for slips and dropped balls. Watch the other team as it takes fielding practice. Who has a strong arm in the outfield? Whose arm might you challenge? File this information away in the back of your mind—you may need it at a key point in the game.

Sound Running Mechanics

You can run faster by using sound running mechanics. Run straight ahead, with your eyes fixed on your destination. Lean forward slightly and run on the balls of your feet. Keep your body neat and compact; your elbows should stay close to your sides. Short, powerful arm pumps will drive your legs even faster.

From Home to First

Once you hit the ball, you're not a batter anymore. You're a runner. So don't stand there admiring your beautiful hit. Run!

Get out of the batter's box as quickly as possible. Take three or four short, quick strides, straighten up, and run all out.

QUICK TIP: How hard you run from home to first on ground balls is a clear indication of how much—or how little—you want to win.

Remember, there's no such thing as a sure out. Even on softly hit ground balls, anything can happen—strange hops, bobbles, bad throws. Always give 100% effort when you run, even if it looks like an easy play. The faster you get down the line, the more

RUN ALL OUT TO FIRST—it's the only base you are allowed to overrun, so don't slow down until after you cross the bag.

pressure you put on the defense to make a quick play. Your effort may force an error.

First base is the only base you are allowed to overrun. Try to step on the front half of the base—it may save a split-second. Also, never slow down until you pass the bag. Once you pass first, turn right into foul territory and come straight back to the bag.

Making the Turn

On a clean single to the outfield, make a wide turn around first and go about 10 feet toward second base. In your mind, you're hoping for a misplay in the field. If the outfielder bobbles the ball, you might be able to turn on the jets and take an extra base.

MAKING THE TURN: Approach the bag by making a gradual curve about 15 feet before the base. Try to step on the inside corner of the base without breaking stride.

Again, *by being an aggressive baserunner, you can force the other team to rush and make errors.*

The proper way to round first base is to run directly toward the base until you are about fifteen feet from the bag. Then make a gradual arc toward the right before turning in toward the bag. This way you can touch the inside corner of the base and head straight toward second. Even if you don't intend to run all the way to second, take a good-sized turn. This aggressive running will put extra pressure on the defense.

One more thing: Listen to your base coach. The coach is there to help you make the right baserunning decisions.

As a Runner on First

You must run on all ground balls. After all, if you stayed on first, there would soon be two runners on the base! (Besides being crowded, it's against the rules.) Therefore, don't hesitate when the batter hits a ground ball. Take off immediately for second base—and be prepared to slide if it's a close play.

On fly balls to the outfield, it's best to drift about halfway between first and second. If the ball is dropped, you'll be on your way. If the fielder catches the ball, quickly return to first, Don't stray too far—it would be a big blunder to get doubled off. Be certain you can get back in plenty of time.

QUICK TIP: If there are two outs, run on anything hit.

As a Runner on Second

With runners on first *and* second, both runners must advance on ground balls. But if you are on second and there isn't a runner on first, you have the option of running or holding your position. In this situation, run to third on all ground balls hit to right side of the infield. If the ball is fielded by the shortstop, pitcher, or third baseman, you should hold your position on second. But be alert, you might be able to race to third immediately after the infielder throws to first.

You have to use your head on fly balls. If it's a deep fly to right, "tag up" (see next page) and race to third the moment the ball hits the fielder's glove. On shallow hits to the outfield, take a short lead off second. But be ready to get back to the bag quickly if the ball is caught. On flies into left or centerfield, go halfway. If the ball falls in for a hit, advance to third. If it's caught, return to second.

On singles, race to third with the thought of making it all the way to home, Look to your third base coach for instructions. He may tell you to slide, to hold up, or try to score. If the coach waves you around, take a good, tight turn and don't look back.

QUICK TIP: Always know the game situation—the number of outs, the score, the inning. It will determine the type of chances you should take.

As a Runner on Third

You must advance on ground balls when the bases are loaded. If you aren't forced, you'll have to make a tough decision whether to run on ground balls. Use your base coach to help you make the right choice. If there are less than two outs, be sure the ball passes the infield before running. But there are many variables to consider. If the ball is hit slowly—and if you have good speed—then it's worth the risk. Be aggressive. If it will take a

49

perfect play to throw you out, odds say you should go for it. Make the other team be perfect. After all, people don't often make perfect plays. Remember, always run from third to home in foul territory, just to the right of the baseline. This way you can't be called for interference if you get in the way of a batted ball.

Tagging Up

With less than two outs, a runner may tag up from any base on balls hit in the air. The odds for success are best on fly balls to the outfield. Chances become even better when the runner is tagging up from third base, because the outfielder has to throw such a long way to home plate.

Brace one foot firmly against the bag, with your body leaning towards home. Watch the fly ball over your shoulder. The moment the ball hits the fielder's glove, push off hard against the base. Pump your arms, keep your eyes fixed on the plate, and be ready to slide. The on-deck batter should be positioned behind home plate. He'll tell you whether to slide or cross the plate standing.

Sliding

The simplest, safest slide to learn is called the bent-knee slide. Your slide should begin about ten feet from the bag. Push off with either leg and tuck it beneath the other leg. In a way, it's almost as if you have suddenly decided to sit down. Your body "slides" on your tucked-in leg and your hip pockets. Make contact with the bag with the sole of your top foot. To avoid injuries, keep your top leg slightly bent, not stiff as a board. It will help absorb the impact of hitting the base.

Sliding is relatively easy, once you get the hang of it. But if you slide incorrectly, you can hurt yourself. Here are three safety

THE BENT-KNEE SLIDE is sometimes called the "Figure 4" slide, because your bent leg and top leg make a shape that resembles the number four.

tips: 1) Don't begin your slide too close to the bag. 2) Never change your mind in the middle of a slide— once you've decided to slide, do it. 3) Don't try to brace your fall by letting your hands touch the ground. This risks an injury to your fingers and hands. Instead hold your hands above your shoulders as you slide.

After you master the bent-knee slide, you may want to ask your coach to teach you some other sliding techniques, such as the fall-away slide, the hook slide, and—if you're a little bit crazy—the head-first slide.

Stealing

In Little League Baseball, *it is against the rules for the runner to leave the base until the pitched ball crosses the plate.* You are not allowed to take a lead off the base. Still, that doesn't rule out steals entirely. It simply makes it more difficult.

Stand with your left foot braced against the edge of the base and your body facing the batter. Your first step is your most

IT'S IMPORTANT TO GET A QUICK START.
Make sure that your first step is a crossover step.
Use your arms to help drive your legs.

important, so make sure it's a crossover step. That is, plant with your right foot and "cross over" with your left foot. Don't make your first step a short jab with your right foot—it doesn't bring you any closer to the next base and wastes precious time. As you push off, keep your body low. Take short, quick steps, pumping with your arms. Straighten up and take longer strides once you gain momentum.

DRILL #5—Slip-sliding Away!

Sliding can be a tricky skill to master. But it can also be a lot of fun to practice...if you use this drill. For starters, find a smooth, slippery surface to practice on. For example, a flattened cardboard refrigerator box is perfect. Take it into the outfield and practice sliding in your stocking feet. Don't run on the box, just slide on it. If you try to run on the cardboard, you could easily slip and hurt yourself.

A long sheet of plastic is another good surface to use. Lay out the strip and wet it down with a hose or a bucket of water. You may even try soaping it down a bit to make the surface even more slippery. It's a fun, safe way to practice sliding—especially on a hot summer's day!

PLAYING THE OUTFIELD

Most of the action might be in the infield, but the outfield is often where the most exciting plays occur. As an outfielder, you'll get fewer chances, but each one will be important. Because if you let a ball get behind you it could easily become a four-base blunder.

Of course, as an outfielder, you may not even touch the ball for several innings. Or perhaps for the entire game. It can be easy to start daydreaming. You have to work at staying "in the game." Think about the hitters. Back up every ball. Anticipate situations. Throughout the game, ask yourself questions such as : "Which base should I throw to if I field a single?" By thinking ahead, you'll be ready for anything. And you'll be glad you did— because anything can happen.

Ready for Anything

When you least expect it, a batter will smack a line drive into the outfield and you'll suddenly be in the middle of the game's biggest play. That's why you've got to be ready on every single pitch.

Position yourself comfortably. You should be ready, but relaxed. Like an infielder, stand with your legs open about shoulder-width and your knees bent. Some outfielders like to stand with one foot a little further back than the other. This gives them an extra edge for balls hit over their head. It's all right to rest your hands on your knees. But don't go to sleep. You've got to be ready to move—right, left, toward the plate, or back.

Catching Flies

Frogs catch flies and so should you. Only your flies are baseballs hit by batters more than 100 feet away. And, of course, you don't use your tongue like a frog would; fortunately, you've got a glove.

At the crack of the bat—or "ping," if the batter uses an aluminum bat—a good outfielder can pretty much tell where the ball has been hit. You'll need to take a lot of practice flies to help you acquire this skill. Run immediately to where you think the

THE BEST POSITION TO CATCH A FLY is with both hands slightly above your forehead, on the same side as your throwing arm. This way you can catch the ball and throw without wasting a second.

ball will descend. Remember to run on the balls of your feet, not your heels. It's much faster and less jarring. Get in position quickly and call for the ball by yelling, "I've got it!" Then, simply wait for the ball to come to you. It should be pointed out that some outfielders like to slowly drift over and catch the ball on the run. That's a good way to make errors. It's also called showing off—something the best outfielders never do. They know that making the play correctly, every time, is the best way for a fielder to truly "show off."

As the ball comes down, stay relaxed and balanced. Let the ball come to you. Keep your feet spread, with your throwing foot slightly back. Your arms should be bent slightly, not stiff as a board. Don't stab at the ball or try to catch it with your arm fully extended. Remember, let the ball come to you. Watch it fall into your glove. And please—use two hands!

Once you're comfortable fielding flies, practice waiting for the ball about one step *behind* where it will actually fall. Then step into the ball as you make your catch. This movement brings your weight forward and saves precious time when you need to get off a quick, powerful throw.

QUICK TIP: Use your glove to shield your eyes from the sun. Turn your body so that you can approach the ball without looking directly into the sun.

Points to Remember

- Always think ahead.
- Be ready for anything.
- Get a good "jump" on the ball.
- Run on the balls of your feet.

- Get under the ball quickly—don't slowly drift to the ball.
- Don't stab at the ball, let it come to you.

Get Rid of the Ball Quickly

Once you've caught the ball, it's important that you quickly return it to the infield.

The key to this is that you are making a change, or *transition*, from a "catcher" to a "thrower." Your first responsibility is to catch the ball. Once that's done, quickly take the ball out of your glove. Get a good grip on it. Fix your eyes on your target and "aim" with your non-throwing shoulder. Now take a quick skip-and-step. Make sure you step toward your target. Your throw should be a low line drive, about chest high. Don't lob it, blob it, or toss it in a high arc. The fastest path between two places is a straight line, or, in this case, a line drive.

Practice this transition over and over again. You can even practice it alone. Toss a short pop into the air. See how quickly you make the transition from "catcher" to "thrower." Just don't get sloppy. Always take enough time to ensure that your throw will be strong and accurate.

Think Ahead of the Game

All too often outfielders waste time getting rid of the ball. This is a result of indecision—they don't know where to throw it. Because their head isn't in the game.

Besides possessing good speed and a strong throwing arm, *outfielders have to think along with the game*. You have to know what the score is, how many runners are on base, how many outs there are, who's up at bat, etc. But you can't stop there—you have to think *ahead* of the game too!

Here is the outfielder's Golden Rule: *Know what to do with the ball before it comes to you.*

The best way to achieve this is by asking yourself questions all game long. Review the game situation in your mind, and then think of possible plays that might occur. For example: It's a tie score, there is one out, runners are on first and third. This is what you may say to yourself: "If it's a short fly, the runner at third will probably tag up. I'll have to be ready to catch the ball and make a strong throw to home as quickly as possible. But if this batter hits a single, the runner at third will score easily. I'll cut off the runner on first from making it all the way to third by quickly throwing to third base."

By thinking ahead like this, you'll be ready for any ball that's hit to you.

Here is another Golden Rule: *Always throw ahead of the lead runner.* The reason is simple. If you throw behind the lead runner, the runner can easily take an extra base. Your job is to hold the runner to the base the runner's already on. If the batter hits a single, throw to second base. On a double, throw to third. If the bases are loaded, throw to home or the cut-off player.

Team Defense

Baseball is a team game. It's won by solid team play, combined with individual effort. Nowhere is this more true than on defense.

Say you've chased after the ball and now have to make a long throw. This is when you use a relay man. A shortstop or second baseman, depending on which outfield position you play, will come out onto the edge of the outfield and call for the ball by holding both hands above the head. The reason teams do this is because it's easier—and faster—to make two short throws than one very long throw. Your job is to throw a line drive to the relay man (or woman!). Aim for the chest area. Then the relay person will catch the ball, turn, and complete the throw. Teamwork like this wins baseball games.

Another sort of relay play is when your defense uses a "cut-off" player. Imagine that a runner is trying to score. Normally, the first baseman (or the third baseman) will act as your "cut-off" player. He will position himself about fifteen feet in front of home plate, in a straight line between the outfielder and home. Your job is to "hit" the cut-off player. It's as if you are trying to throw a hard line drive "through" his head! This way he has the option of letting the ball go through to the catcher for a play at the plate...or cutting it off. If he cuts it off, he can either complete the throw himself, throw to another base, or hold on to the ball.

Points to Remember

- Think ahead of the game—anticipate where to throw the ball *before* it comes to you.
- Get rid of the ball quickly.
- Always throw ahead of the lead runner.
- Throw "through" the cut-off player with a line drive about chest high.

Fielding Grounders

If an infielder lets a grounder go between his legs, it's a one-base error. But if an outfielder goofs up, well...it's big trouble. You've got to make sure grounders don't get past you.

If there are no runners on and a batter hits a single, here's what you should do. First, charge the ball quickly. Slow down as you near the ball. It's best to get down on one knee in front of the ball to make sure it doesn't get past you. On most singles, you'll

GET DOWN ON ONE KNEE FOR GROUNDERS
when no runners are on base. Be sure to get in
front of the ball, keep your glove low, and watch
the ball all the way into your glove.

have enough time to make this play. Keep your glove low to the
ground; it's easier to come up for the ball than to come down.
Keep your head down too—this way it's natural for you to *follow
the ball with your eyes into the glove.* Once you have the ball,
don't waste a second. Get up quickly, take a quick skip, and fire
the ball into second base.

With runners in scoring position, you'll need to get off a hard,
accurate throw as quickly as possible. You won't have the luxury
of getting down on one knee. In this case, charge the ball, slowing
up slightly as you draw close. Bend at the waist and knees to
catch the ball with your glove near the side of your non-throwing
foot. But don't rush and take risks unless you're reasonably sure
you can make the play. Now come up throwing in one, smooth,
fluid motion. Use the forward momentum you already have to

1.

2.

3.

4.

TRY TO MAKE YOUR
CATCH AND THROW IN
ONE SMOOTH MOTION.
When you have to throw
a runner out, charge the
ball, catch it near your
non-throwing foot, and
come up gunning. Step
toward your target and
execute a strong follow
through.

generate a strong throw. A good follow through will give you more power and greater accuracy. During practice, you might try exaggerating your follow through by touching your back with your throwing hand. This will get you into the habit of putting your whole body into the throw.

Points to Remember

- Follow the ball with your eyes into the glove.
- On ground singles with no runners on, you should get down on one knee.
- With runners on, charge, bend, and come up throwing in one, smooth motion.
- Step toward the target and follow through—put your whole body into the throw.

Positioning

Each outfield position demands slightly different skills from each player. A right fielder should have the best arm, because he's got the longest throw to third base. The center fielder should be the fastest runner—he has the most ground to cover. And the left fielder should have a good, reliable glove, because so many righty batters pull the ball into left field.

When it comes to positioning, there are several things to consider. First off, position yourself where you have a clear view of the batter. You should also know that most batters tend to pull the ball. That is, right-handed batters "pull" the ball across their body, hitting it to the left side of the field. Left-handed batters "pull" the ball to the right side of the field. For instance, if you're in centerfield and a lefty batter comes up, you should shift toward right field.

Generally speaking, though, the best guide is to know as much as you can about the batter, the pitcher, the abilities of your teammates, and the field conditions. If your pitcher throws very fast, most batters will swing late; their balls will usually go to the opposite field. Also notice where foul balls go. If the batter pulls one down the line, take a few steps closer to the line. The key is, think along with the game. Make adjustments according to each new situation.

Hey, Talk It Up Out There!

Chatter, or "talking it up," is a part of the game. And it's not just noise. It's a useful way of keeping yourself, and your teammates, focused on the game.

If a batter comes up and you remember what he did last time, share that information with your teammates. Yell to your leftfielder, "Hey, he pulled the ball into left last time up. Heads up out there."

Communication is most important on pop-ups when more than one fielder can catch the ball. To avoid injuries or needless errors, players must call for the ball. When you are sure you can catch

CALL FOR THE BALL by waving your arms and yelling, loud enough for everyone to hear, "I've got it! I've got it!" Then...make sure you get it.

64

the ball, wave your arms and yell, loud and clear, "I've got it. I've got it!" The other fielders will give you plenty of room to make the catch. However, if someone else calls for the ball *after* you've called for it, then it's their ball. The second player to call for the ball is always the one who should take it. On pop-ups that are between the infield and the outfield, the outfielder should make the catch whenever possible. It's the outfielder's ball because it's easier to move in for the ball than it is to move back.

Back Each Other Up

The great thing about being on a team is that you're not all alone out there. You have teammates who will help each other out for the sake of the team.

You do this by backing each other up. As an outfielder, you should back up every grounder that's hit to the infield. If the infielder makes an error, you'll be there to hold it to a single. Likewise, outfielders need to back up each other. If there's a fly to left, the centerfielder should run toward the ball and be ready to help out if the player has problems fielding the ball. If a ball is hit into the gap, back up the play. Look to the infield to check the runners. Help the player with the ball know where to throw it. Yell, "Third!" or "Home!" Little things like backing up can mean a lot. It's what teamwork is all about.

Points to Remember

- Make adjustments in your position throughout the game for each new situation.
- Stay focused on the game—talk it up!
- Call for the ball, loud and clear, when—and only when— you are sure you'll catch it.
- Play as a team. Back up each play.

65

DRILL #6—The Crossover Step

The toughest play for an outfielder is when a ball is hit over your head. Here's a simple drill that will help you: 1) locate pop-ups and flyballs; 2) go back on the ball by making a "crossover step"; and 3) return the ball to the infield quickly.

Go to an area where you have plenty of room. Stand about 30 feet away from a teammate. Take turns tossing pop-ups over each other's heads. Throw them to the right, to the left, and directly overhead.

To catch these balls, it's essential that you have a quick first step. The quickest step for an outfielder is the crossover step. This simple technique is used in many facets of the game—in the

THE CROSSOVER STEP should be used in all facets of play—running the bases, infield, and outfield play.

infield, on the basepaths, and in the outfield. You'll do well to master it.

If the ball is thrown over your head to the right, pivot on both feet, *then* make your first step with your *left* foot across your body. (If the ball's to your left, step with your right foot.) Keeping your eye on the ball all the way, run back in an angle to where the ball will land.

By "crossing over" with your first step, you are avoiding the common mistake of the "jab step." A jab step is when, in the same situation, your first step is a short jab with your *right* foot. This jab wastes valuable time—and doesn't bring you any closer to the ball.

Once you catch the ball with both hands, quickly get a grip on it, get set, and throw the ball on a line drive to your teammate. Remember, *a quick release is just as important as a strong arm*. Take turns fielding pop-ups until the cross-over step becomes second nature to you.

THE ART OF PITCHING

It's the bottom of the sixth inning and your team is leading, 3-2. There are two outs—only one more to go. But the bases are loaded and the other team's best hitter is at the plate. You stand on the pitching rubber and concentrate on the catcher's target. You take a deep breath and grip the ball in your glove. All eyes focus on you. And of course, they should. The game is literally in your hands.

No position on the field rivals the importance of pitcher. But along with that importance, comes responsibility. You must strive to perform to the best of your ability. On every pitch, you put your entire body to the test. You drive with your legs, turn with your hips, bend with your back—and, most importantly, use your head.

A Matter of Control

Consistency...concentration...confidence. All pitchers must possess these characteristics. But if the key to pitching can be summed up in one word, it would have to be this: *Control.*

If you have control, then consistency, concentration, and confidence will soon follow. But control, for a pitcher, means more than the ability to throw strikes. You must "control the situation" by mastering your emotions. No matter what happens, you have to try to stay calm and focused. If someone hits a homer, you can't get upset. You must remain poised and concentrate on the job in front of you—making a good pitch to the *next* batter.

How do you make yourself concentrate? By "controlling your mind," thinking about the task at hand. Free your mind of distractions. It's as if you are in a long tunnel. You stand at one end, the catcher's mitt is at the other. When you are in your pitching motion, only the "tunnel" matters. All of your attention should be fixed on the catcher's glove.

What's more, the key to throwing strikes is having a consistent windup. Your body goes through the exact same motions on every pitch. In other words, you must "control your body" in order to control the ball.

QUICK TIP: The key to pitching can be summed up in one word—control.

The Windup

A strong, consistent windup is essential for successful pitching. A windup gives you rhythm and momentum. This momentum helps you throw the ball harder. However, there is no standard windup to recommend. There are many, many variations. One way to develop your own unique windup is to begin by imitating a few favorite Major League pitchers. As you practice different windups you'll gradually find your natural groove. As a general rule: *If it doesn't feel right, then it probably isn't right for you.*

The Stance

Concentrate on the catcher's target and think about the pitch you are about to make. One or both feet must be on the pitching rubber. You should be loose and relaxed, facing home plate. Take a deep breath. You may prefer to hold the ball in your throwing hand behind your back. The less the batter sees the ball, the better.

Stepping Back

This stage is often called the "rocker step" because you begin your motion by *rocking* back. This move is like turning the key of an engine—it provides the momentum you need to move forward with power.

Step a few inches straight back with your glove side foot. Bring your hands up toward your chest. (Note: If you prefer, you may bring them all the way over your head.)

Remember, *the first half of your windup should be slow and easy.*

The Pivot

Turn on the ball of your front foot until it is even with the pitching rubber. Your foot should be immediately in front of the rubber, not on it. It must remain in contact with the rubber.

Your hips and shoulders also turn; you actually show the batter your hip pocket. All of your weight is still back, balanced on your "throwing" leg. It's critically important to keep your balance here. Don't rush—stay smooth, cool, and collected.

Driving Forward

Now your windup begins to build speed. You break your hands and extend your throwing arm behind your body. You drive off the rubber, pushing hard with your throwing leg.

A consistent stride is important to your control. Your front foot should hit the same spot on the mound every time. Step forward on the ball of your foot, not the heel. And be sure not to over-

THE TOTAL MOTION: Your windup should be a smooth, easy motion. However, this one motion is actually a series of interlocking stages.

You can see each stage in this series of photos.

extend yourself by striding too far. At this point, your hips and shoulders are beginning to turn.

Chest and Hip Turn

Bang—here's the moment of explosiveness in your motion. So far you've been nice and easy. But now you've just pushed hard off the rubber. It's time to make a quick, powerful turn with your hips and shoulders to face the plate. Drive your chest directly toward the plate. This rapid movement brings your entire body behind the pitch. Your elbow is up, parallel with your throwing shoulder and your arm is whipping forward, nearing the release point.

The Delivery and Follow Through

With your arm extended and your weight forward, you release the ball. But your work's not done yet. You must finish with a strong follow through.

For maximum power, "bury" your throwing shoulder in the ground and swing your arm across your body. Your back is bent, nearly parallel to the ground. The force of this movement will lift your pivot foot up off the ground. Let it swing forward. Balance on the balls of your feet and bring your hands forward—be prepared to field all balls that are hit back to you.

Points to Remember

- Your windup should begin slowly...and speed up toward the end.
- Begin by concentrating on the catcher's glove.
- Rock back before moving forward.
- Pivot by turning your foot, hips, and shoulders—show the batter your hip pocket.

- Drive forward by pushing hard off the rubber.
- Explode into a quick, powerful hip and shoulder turn as you face the batter.
- Throw the ball with your arm fully extended.
- Follow through by "burying" your shoulder and bending your back. Be ready to field the ball.

The Fastball

The heater, the hummer, the bread-and-butter pitch. Smoke, fire, gas. Whatever you call it, the fastball is the best way to stretch and strengthen young arms. Every pitcher must be able to throw a hard, accurate fastball. Yes, as you get older, a variety of off-speed pitches (curve, slider, changeup) will help you keep batters off-balance—but only if you have a fastball worth worrying about.

At this stage in your development, the fastball is the only pitch you should throw. Too many young, talented pitchers have *permanently damaged* their arms by throwing curveballs at too young an age. The important thing is to build up your technique, your arm strength, and your control. The best and only way to accomplish that is by throwing fastballs.

The basic grip to throw a fastball is with two fingers across the seams, with the thumb underneath, also on a seam. This grip gives you better control and provides backspin on the ball as you release it. However, each pitcher likes to grip the fastball a slightly different way. You should experiment with different grips. For example, try holding the ball along the seams. Many pitchers claim this puts more movement on the ball, making it trail off to the side. The bad news is that it's a tougher pitch to control.

> QUICK TIP: Throwing a fastball is the best way to stretch and strengthen your arm.

Grip the ball loosely with the ends of your fingers, as if you were holding a soft tomato. Don't jam the ball too far back into your hand. Keep your hands and wrist as relaxed as possible. You'll need a loose wrist to get that extra snap, crackle, and pop on your fastball.

Working the Batter

If you are a pitcher—and if you'd like to *stay* a pitcher—then you must be able to consistently throw strikes.

When you walk a batter, you give that batter a free pass to first base. The batter hasn't *earned* anything—you *gave* it to him. That's why so many managers say "make the batter hit the ball." You've got eight other players on the field to help you out. You do your job; let your fielders do theirs.

Another advantage to throwing strikes is that you put the batter in a hole. Think about it. When batters are behind in the count, 0-1, or 0-2, they begin to think defensively. They think, "Oh no— I hope I don't strike out." This negative thinking causes batters to lose confidence. And when you take away a batter's confidence, it's almost as good as taking the bat out of his hands.

On the other hand, if you start off by throwing balls, you are digging a hole for yourself! Now you're the one thinking negatively ("I'd better not walk this guy") and the batter is thinking nothing but good thoughts. Visions of home runs dance in his head. He knows you'll have to throw a strike, so he'll look for a pitch right down the middle. And he'll be sure to take a good rip at it.

QUICK TIP: Stay ahead of the batter by throwing strikes—it gives you a tremendous advantage over the batter.

The best pitchers have excellent control. But they not only control balls and strikes, they control *where* the strikes are located—inside, outside, high, or low. They avoid throwing "fat" strikes right down the middle.

As a general rule, it's best to keep the ball low, right around the batter's knees. For most hitters, low pitches are the most difficult to hit. However, you should vary your pitches. For example, on your first two pitches to a batter, throw the ball inside and low. Then, just when he's getting used to seeing the ball inside, throw a fastball just off the outside part of the plate. By using the entire plate, you'll keep batters off-balance.

Once you've mastered throwing strikes consistently, it's time for the next lesson—learning how *not* to throw strikes! As you know, not all batters are disciplined hitters. Some will swing at anything, even at balls *over* their head! If a free-swinging batter comes to the plate, you don't want to throw pitches he can hit. Try to get a quick strike on the batter with your first pitch. Now that you've got the batter in a hole, you can really start working on him. Throw the next pitch *below* his knees...or just outside the plate. If you can entice the batter to swing at a bad pitch, it will make your job that much easier.

Suppose the other team's big home run hitter is up. See if you can get him to go "fishing" for the ball. Throw a big, fat, juicy, extra-slow pitch...*about one foot outside the plate*. The batter's eyes will light up, he'll take a mighty swing, and he'll hit nothing but air. After all, it's tough to hit what you can't reach.

Making Adjustments

Just as fielders must make adjustments in their positioning throughout the game, you've also got to make adjustments. The key to making these adjustments is becoming your own pitching coach. You must know yourself. You've got to recognize your mistakes...and learn how to correct them.

If your pitches don't seem to be going where you want them to, the fault probably lies with your pitching mechanics. Review in your mind the characteristics of a successful windup. Are you flustered or upset by a fielder's error? Remember that a windup begins with a calm, relaxed pitcher. Gather your thoughts by taking a short stroll off the mound. Give the ball a rub, take a deep breath, and focus on what you need to do.

If you start getting tired, you may have difficulty keeping the ball down. This is probably because you aren't following through properly. Make the adjustment you need to pitch well. Really bury your throwing shoulder after each pitch. Make sure you bend your back. Just a little fine-tuning will do the trick.

One last flaw to discuss is created for a very good reason—you are trying too hard. Sometimes, when you try very hard, it does more harm than good. You try to make each pitch perfect. You overthrow the ball. And you lose your natural rhythm. Professional baseball players have a phrase they use when a player tries to do too much. They say, "He isn't *staying within himself.*" Keep in mind that your pitching motion should be loose and fluid. Think calm thoughts. Try to find your groove again. Ease into your pitching motion. Gently rock back, pivot, extend your arm, and drive forward. It should be one, almost effortless, motion.

Points to Remember

- Grip a fastball loosely, as if you were holding a ripe tomato.
- Throw strikes, throw strikes, throw strikes!
- Vary the location of your pitches—up, down, inside, outside.
- Attack a batter's weakness; make adjustments on the mound.

- Stay within yourself—sometimes when you try too hard it only makes things worse.

Fielding the Position

After you release the ball, you instantly become another fielder on the diamond. You must be ready to field balls hit right back up the middle. Make sure that after each pitch you are on the balls of your feet, with your hands in front of you, ready for anything—remember, you're only 40 feet away from home plate! You should be able to charge in for bunts and slow rollers, quickly run to your right or left, and even jump straight up for high choppers.

One of your main responsibilities is covering first base when a ground ball or bunt pulls the first baseman away from the bag. Whenever the ball is hit to the right side of the field, your first move should be to cover first base. Run toward the foul line—about 10 feet before first base. As you near the

BE READY TO FIELD YOUR POSITION after each pitch.

line, turn toward first. Give the first baseman a clear, chest-high target with your glove. Make the catch and step on the bag. Be careful, though—this play can cause a collision between you and the runner. Step on the inside corner of the bag and turn left, towards the infield. This will help you avoid injuries and put you in position to check other baserunners.

Another important way for you to help your team is by backing up. On a play to second, for example, stand about 15 feet behind the bag just in case there's an overthrow. The same with plays to third or home. Lastly, you must be especially alert for passed balls when there is a runner at third. If the ball gets behind the catcher, you must immediately race in to cover home. The catcher will scurry to retrieve the ball...the runner will be speeding home...and you've got to get in position to take the throw and make the tag. Position yourself on the infield side of home plate. *Remember, you can't block the runner from home plate*. Give the catcher a low target. Reach for the ball and slap down the tag. Bang—got 'em!

DRILL #7—Working on Control

Since good control is the single, most important quality for a young pitcher, that's what you should work on the most. And the only way to do that is by pitching.

Find an old, used, thick blanket. With thick tape, mark off a strike zone for a fairly small hitter. Seventeen inches wide, and, say, about two feet high. Depending upon where you live, hang this blanket on a clothes line in your back yard...in front of your garage...or wherever you can find an appropriate spot. The pitcher's mound is exactly 46 feet from home; measure this distance from the blanket and mark it off. Welcome to your new pitching mound.

A wonderful alternative to the blanket is to purchase a "pitch-back" from a sports store. Though there are several types of "pitch-backs" on the market, each is essentially the same. That is, a large net complete with a strike zone, held to a metal frame by springs. This way, the ball will bounce back at you—so you can work on your pitching and your fielding at the same time!

CATCHING

Which player has to be quick as a cat, strong as an ox, crafty as a fox, stubborn as a mule—and play with the heart of a lion?

A catcher, of course! Because a good catcher possesses a rare blend of talents. Tough and smart, the catcher is a team leader. A player who combines outstanding skills with a deep knowledge of the game. The catcher has to be able to work with the pitchers...and outsmart hitters. A catcher has to be both a cheerleader...and an on-field manager.

It's not an easy position—and not everyone's cut out for it. But all of the best catchers have pride in themselves and pride in their position. Maybe that's why catchers are called "the glue of the defense."

Play It Safe

A catcher must learn how to "play it safe" by using the right equipment.

Fortunately, many years of research have gone into providing the catcher with everything he needs to be well-protected behind the plate. This equipment must be worn every game, every inning, every pitch. Don't get careless; your safety is important.

Shin Guards: These guards protect your knees, shins, and ankles from being hit by the ball. When you squat down into position,

YOUR EQUIP-MENT PRO-TECTS YOU when you are facing the pitcher. Don't turn your head or your body to the side—that's when injuries can occur.

make sure that your shin guards are facing the pitcher—not twisted around to the side.

Chest Protector: This soft, flexible material protects your chest, your shoulders and—if it has a lower flap—your groin area.

Helmet and Mask: This equipment gives your head plenty of protection. But like all catcher's equipment, it is designed to protect you when you are facing the pitcher. A face mask can't protect you if you turn your head to the side. Spend time adjusting your mask so that it fits perfectly. It should be snug and firm on your head, yet loose enough for you to pull it off in a hurry.

Athletic Supporter and Cup: All boys, no matter which position they play, should wear an athletic supporter. Catchers should definitely supplement this protection by also wearing a cup beneath their athletic supporter.

Take Your Position

Since most batters are righties, most catchers are also right-handed. That's because of the difficulty lefties have trying to throw to second base when a right-handed batter is at the plate. It may not be fair to southpaws, but that's the way it is. Nevertheless, it's still possible for lefties to make fine catchers. Your biggest problem may be finding a left-handers catcher's mitt!

Take your position by squatting behind the plate, about an arm's length from the batter. If you're concerned with getting hit by the bat, ask the batter to take a slow practice swing. Position yourself accordingly. Get as comfortable as you can in your stance. You should be balanced and stable. Many catchers find it comfortable to squat with their right foot back slightly, pointing toward first base.

Give your pitcher a good target. Since the pitcher is throwing to your glove, you must make the best target possible. Hold your mitt open and in front of your body, with your arm outstretched. If you want the pitcher to work the batter inside or outside, shift your entire body in that direction.

Keep your throwing hand in a fist. One of the most common injuries occurs when catchers get their throwing hand nicked by a foul ball. Avoid this by keeping your throwing hand clenched in a fist, protected behind your glove. Your elbows should be outside your knees; this gives you extra mobility.

Points to Remember

- Wear your equipment every time you get behind the plate—even during practice.
- Position yourself an arm's length from the batter.

- Take a balanced, comfortable squatting position.
- Hold your glove outstretched in front of your body; keep your elbows outside of your knees.
- Be sure to give your pitcher a good target.
- Protect your fingers from injury by keeping your throwing hand in a fist.

KEEP YOUR DISTANCE FROM THE BATTER: If the bat hits your glove, it's catcher's interference. Note: With no runners on base you may hold your throwing hand behind your back.

Work With Your Pitcher

As a catcher, you are in partnership with your pitcher. In one way of thinking, a Little League game is just you and the pitcher having catch. Therefore, it's important that you know your pitcher's strengths and weaknesses. During the game, you should constantly assess your pitcher. Is he working too fast? Is he upset? Is he not following through properly and throwing the ball too high? It's your job to know. Talk to the pitcher. Give encouragement. If you've spotted a weakness, share it with the pitcher. By working as a team, you'll get better results.

COMMUNICATION: Sometimes a pitcher needs a shot of confidence. In key situations, go out to the mound and say, "Come on, let's get this guy. I know you can do it."

Throwing

It takes more than a good arm to throw a runner out. It takes anticipation, quickness, agility, and accuracy. In other words, *technique*. If you learn to throw the right way—the fastest way—then you'll always be a step ahead of the runner.

The key is learning how to make a strong throw without taking many steps. *(Note: Sorry lefties, but this play is described for righty catchers.)*

Pretend you've just caught a pitch and the runner is trying to steal second base. Assume the catching position, with the ball already in your glove. Quickly spring up; bring your left foot forward while pivoting on your right foot. Your knees should be bent, with your non-throwing shoulder and hip aimed at your target. Your feet are about twelve inches apart, with most of your weight on your back leg. At the same time, bring your glove and throwing hand together near your throwing shoulder. Get a good grip on the ball and extend your throwing arm away from your body. Take one step toward your target. Throw the ball straight overhand, snapping down with your wrist as you release it. Follow through by bending forward with your back. Practice this procedure until you can consistently get off a quick, strong throw.

Strive for a throw that stays on a low line drive all the way to the target. A perfect throw should be aimed at the fielder's knees. This way the fielder can slap down a quick tag. Be careful not to step on home as you make your throw. You could easily slip and lose your balance.

BRING BOTH HANDS TO YOUR THROWING SHOULDER: Then extend your arm, step forward, and "snap off" a hard, low throw.

Points to Remember

- Aim with your non-throwing shoulder.
- Bring both hands back to your throwing shoulder.
- Transfer your weight from your back leg to the front leg by stepping forward.
- Snap off the throw with a downward motion of your wrist.
- Follow through—try to make a strong, low throw.

Blocking Balls in the Dirt

If a ball gets past the catcher with a runner on base, the runner will probably advance to the next base. That's why it's so important for catchers to keep balls in front of them.

The first thing to remember about blocking balls is that you're wearing protective equipment. Use it. You don't always have to catch the ball with your glove. In fact, sometimes it's better to use your body.

On pitches that are in the dirt directly in front of you, quickly drop down to both knees with your glove on the ground. Hold the glove so your fingers are pointing downward. Tuck your chin in and keep your head down. This will prevent a ball from bouncing up and hitting you in the throat. Remember, don't turn your head to the side. After blocking the pitch, flip off your mask and immediately get the ball. You'll need cat-like reflexes if you hope to hold the runner.

QUICK TIP: Keep your shoulders even with the pitching rubber. This way the ball will bounce in front of you, not way off to the side.

89

BLOCKING BALLS TO THE SIDE: Take a short jab step with your outside leg and fall to the side. Quickly get your body in front of the ball.

Plays at the Plate

As a catcher, you are the last line of defense. At no time is that more true than on close plays at the plate. The difference of a few seconds will decide whether the runner is safe or out.

A CLOSE PLAY AT THE PLATE: It's the most exciting play in baseball!

With a runner racing to the plate, you've got to be in position to take the throw and make a quick tag. Stand in front of the plate, toward the third base side. Catch the ball with your legs balanced directly beneath your shoulders and your knees bent. Catch the ball with two hands. Sweep down toward the oncoming runner and make the tag by allowing the runner to slide into your glove. Be sure to hold the ball with both hands. Don't let the runner's foot jar the ball loose.

SAFETY TIP: When a play at the plate develops, always take a moment to remove the hitter's bat if it's been left near the baseline or plate area. A stray bat can easily cause a sprained or broken ankle.

ON FORCE PLAYS, pretend you are a first baseman. Step on the base with one foot and step toward the ball with the other. Catch the ball with both hands.

Force Plays

Force plays are a bit easier, because you don't have to tag the runner. Instead, like a first baseman, you must merely step on home with the ball in your possession before the runner reaches the plate.

The key is being absolutely sure that it is, in fact, a force play. *If the runners are not forced, then you must make a tag.* For example, let's say there are runners at second and third. It's a tie game. The batter hits a grounder to the pitcher, who throws it home to you. In this case, you must make a tag, because the runners aren't "forced" to go to the next base. However, if the bases are loaded, it's a force play.

For force plays, take off your mask and stand on home plate with one foot—similar to the way a first baseman takes a throw. Make a good target, about chest level, with your glove. While keeping one foot on the plate, step toward the ball. Catch it with two hands. Quickly step off the plate toward the infield and be ready to throw to another base if necessary.

Points to Remember

- Get your body in front of the ball on pitches in the dirt.
- Be sure to hold the ball with both hands on tag plays.
- Learn to anticipate plays *before* they happen.
- Learn the difference between force outs and tag plays.

Foul Balls and Pop-ups

On a foul ball or pop-up, quickly pull off your mask and try to locate the ball. Hold the mask until you've found the ball. This way you'll avoid tripping over it as you make the play. Once you know approximately where the ball will land, throw the mask in the opposite direction.

To help you locate pop-ups quickly, you should know two things. First, a large percentage of foul balls go to the batter's open side. In other words, in front of the batter. It's your best bet to look in that direction first. Secondly, most pop-ups have a reverse spin. That means the ball will curve back towards the field as you go after it.

On pop-ups behind, or near the plate, it's your ball. If the pop-up drifts up either baseline, it's probably easier for the first baseman or third baseman to make the play.

It's best to catch the ball just above eye level, near your forehead. When the ball hits your glove, cover it with your free hand. Otherwise, it might pop out of your glove.

HOLD THE MASK IN YOUR HAND until you've located the ball. Then— and only then—toss the mask to an area far from where the ball will come down.

Fielding Bunts

You must move quickly, like a cat, to field a bunt. That's why you should be on the balls of your feet when you are in your stance. If you lean back on your heels, it's impossible to get a quick "jump" on the ball.

You should learn to recognize bunt situations. Try to think along with the opposing manager. If there's a runner at first, the manager may put on a sacrifice bunt. Likewise, if a speedy runner is at the plate, you should be aware of the possibility of a bunt. Keep your teammates alert, too. This mental preparation will give you the edge you'll need to make a quick play.

On a sacrifice bunt, you'll have to make a quick decision about which base to throw the ball. It's great if you can get the sure out. Approach the ball with your body in line with the base to which you'll throw. To do so, you may need to half-circle the ball before picking it up.

FIELD THE BUNT WITH BOTH HANDS. Bring your body low to the ball by bending with your knees and back. Then rise up, get set, and make a quick, overhand throw.

Even if another player fields the ball, you can help your teammates by telling them where to throw the ball. Remember, as a catcher, you have the best view of the field.

DRILL #8—Scouting the Hitters

One of the most important skills for a catcher to develop is learning to recognize the strengths and weaknesses of various hitters.

So here's your drill: Go to a Little League game, sit directly behind the backstop, and watch. Go alone. Quietly study the hitters. Notice how they stand at the plate. Do they crowd it? What kind of stride do they take? If they step into the bucket, you'll know to pitch them outside. Study their swing. Do they ever bunt? Are they sluggers? Notice, especially, when they swing and miss. Where was the pitch? Make a mental note of it and use the information at a later date.

The real purpose of this drill is to get you thinking about the game. Yes, catching is much more than back-breaking

95

labor. It's a position for thinkers. So forget your shin guards, your mitt, and your mask. Make use of the most valuable equipment you've got. That's right—Brain Power!

THE INFIELD: FIRST, SECOND, SHORT AND THIRD

Unless your Little League team has a pitcher who can strike out every batter, you absolutely must have a solid, dependable infield. Most coaches agree: They would rather have a steady, if unspectacular player in the infield than a sensational, but error-prone, fielder.

Remember, *routine plays performed well do more to help a team win than the rare "spectacular" play.*

The single most important skill for an infielder—whether you play first, second, short, or third—is the ability to catch ground balls. Let's begin by looking at this skill. Then we'll consider the responsibilities of each position one at a time.

Fielding Grounders

Fielding a grounder and throwing to first in time to get the runner is a complicated task. It involves quickness, dexterity, coordination, fluidity, sure-handedness, and a good throwing arm. Even when you execute the play perfectly, you may only nip the runner by a step.

On Your Toes

More balls are hit to the infield than to the outfield. And though you may go innings without touching the ball, you have

TAKE A *SHORT* STEP TOWARD THE PLATE as the pitcher goes into the windup. Bring both hands forward, in front of your body. Note: You should actually take a shorter step than pictured here.

to be ready for every pitch. Begin by taking a relaxed stance. Your feet are spread, your attention is focused on the batter. It's okay, at this point, to rest your hands on your knees. But as the pitcher begins the windup, bring your hands forward and take a short step toward the plate. This technique brings your weight to the balls of your feet and places you in total readiness. You're on your toes, ready to get a quick jump on the ball.

Charge the Ball

Charge ground balls whenever possible. This will give you more time to field the ball, get set, and make a strong throw. If you back up on the ball—or if you wait for a slow roller to come to you—the runner will have a much better chance of reaching first safely.

Get in Front of the Ball

Without a doubt, the best way to field grounders is to get in front of the ball. Here's where smooth, quick footwork really pays off. All too often errors occur when fielders try to catch the ball to the side of their body. Yes, there are times when you must make a backhand play or even dive for the ball. But in all cases, do everything you can to field the ball in front of you.

Balanced and Ready

Think of yourself as a human sponge. You are trying to absorb all the balls that are hit to you. Watch the hop of the ball as it comes toward you. Get set to catch it by positioning yourself on a balanced base. Your feet are spread, your knees bent, your rear end is down, and your glove is lightly brushing the ground. That's essential—if your glove doesn't get dirty, then you aren't holding it low enough. It's easier to bring your glove up to field a grounder than it is to stab it downward at the last moment.

> QUICK TIP: Many errors occur when fielders hold their bodies too stiffly. Bend at the knees and the waist—*get your body and your glove close to the ground.* After all, they're called "grounders."

Soft Hands

Keep your nose pointed at the ball until it hits your glove. This way you'll be sure to keep your head down and focused on the ball. Of course, use both hands whenever possible.

As always when you catch a ball, try to cushion it. Don't stab at the ball; gently absorb the grounder by pulling your hands back slightly as you catch it. This is called "soft hands"—a quality all of the best fielders possess.

Make the Throw

Now that you've caught the ball, you need to make a smooth transition to the throwing position. First, bring both hands together near your belt buckle. Rise up and turn your eyes toward your target. Aim with your non-throwing shoulder and hip. Balance, as in all aspects of baseball, is key. You must always field and throw from a firm base. Plant your back foot before attempting to throw. Grip the ball and bring it out of the glove to make an overhand throw. Step forward and follow through. To put extra mustard on your throw, use the skip-and-step method discussed in the chapter, "Catching and Throwing the Baseball."

The Backhand Catch

Of course, you can't always get in front of the ball. Going to your right to make a backhand catch is a true test of your ability. It's a play that requires daily practice. As you move to the right, keep your eye on the ball at all times. Backhand the ball and come to a full stop by bracing on your right foot. Then, turn and throw overhand by pushing off your right foot and stepping toward your target.

QUICK TIP: Even if you can't make the throw to first, try to knock the ball down and keep it from rolling into the outfield.

Points to Remember

- Bring your hands forward and your weight to the balls of your feet.
- Charge the ball—don't wait for it to come to you.
- Get in front of the ball.
- Hold your glove low to the ground.
- Watch the ball all the way into your glove.
- Plant and throw from a firm base.

Playing First Base

Besides the pitcher and catcher, the first baseman fields more balls than any player on the team. It's a position that demands a sure glove and a "heads-up" approach to the game. In addition, first base is the only infield position, besides pitcher, that's appropriate for left-handed players.

101

1.

In this series, the infielder follows many of the Golden Rules for fielding ground balls: He's balanced and ready. He gets himself in front of the ball. He bends down for the ball and carries his glove low to the ground. He watches the ball

2.

3.

4.

5.

into his glove. He uses both hands. He absorbs the ball by bringing it up to his belt buckle. He plants his foot and throws from a firm base.

6.

Positioning

In the beginning, you may be worried about getting back to first base in time to take the throw. That's why many Little Leaguers are reluctant to stray more than a few feet from the bag. However, the best fielding first basemen stop a lot of balls from getting through to the outfield by covering a good-sized area of the field. They don't hesitate to stray a little from the bag, because they know they can get back in time to take the throw. Of course, you can't stray *too* far. As you play, you'll gradually get comfortable with the position. You'll learn that you cover more area by playing "off the bag."

Taking the Throw

On a ground ball, it's your responsibility to take the throw at first base for the out. As soon as it's hit, hustle over to the bag.

TAKING THE THROW: Avoid injuries—don't stand directly on the bag. You'll be in the runner's way and may cause a collision. One foot on the edge of the bag is far safer.

Face the fielder who has the ball, giving a chest-high target with your glove. Here's where good footwork is important. Stand with the back heels of your feet against the bag. Make your catch by stepping toward the ball with one foot, *keeping your other foot on the edge of the bag*. Which foot you step with depends upon the throw. If the ball is to your right, step with your right foot. If it's to your left, step with your left foot. Of course, you must be touching the bag for the runner to be called out. However, *your first responsibility is the ball—you must make every effort to catch the ball even if you have to leave first base to handle a poor throw*. It doesn't help your team if you manage to keep your foot on the bag...and the ball goes sailing past you!

Points to Remember

- Don't play too close to the bag. Stay a few feet behind the bag and a few feet from the foul line.
- Always give a good, chest-high target.
- Reach for the ball by stepping toward the ball with one foot—keep the other foot on the bag!
- Your first responsibility is catching the ball—even if that means leaving first base to catch a poor throw.

Talk It Up

All infielders should talk it up, calling out encouragement to the team. It's an important way of helping yourself—and your teammates—stay in the game and on the ball. But the first baseman seems to play an especially vital role in this area. Perhaps it's because of your nearness to the pitcher. Or, simply because the first baseman is often a team leader. Whatever the reason, you can solidify your defense by talking it up. After each play, let your teammates know how many outs there are. If you suspect a bunt, say so. If a fielder makes a nice play, be the first one to give praise. If a player makes an error, tell him, "That's all right, we'll get the next one."

The Underhand Toss

Sometimes you'll be forced to range far from first base to field a ground ball. In these cases, you may not be able to beat the runner in a foot race to the bag. Fortunately, the pitcher should be covering first base for you. When you are close to your target, it's best to toss the ball underhand. Take the ball out of your glove right away. This gives the pitcher a clear view of the ball. Then, like a bowler, step toward your target and toss the ball in a low arc toward the pitcher's chest.

THE UNDERHAND TOSS: Hold the ball in clear view for the pitcher to see it. Then step toward your target and toss the ball in a low arc. Your throw should reach the pitcher just *before* he steps on the bag, at about chest-level.

Pop-ups

Call for pop-ups by yelling, "I've got it, I've got it." But don't call for the ball unless you are sure you can, in fact, get it. To be safe, you should wait until the ball reaches its highest point before calling for it. You should take all pop-ups near first base, in foul territory, and all the way toward home plate on your side of the diamond. It's an easier play for the second baseman to catch pop flies hit behind you. Go for the ball, but listen for your second baseman. If he calls you off, get out of the way.

Bunts

If you suspect a bunt, slowly creep toward the plate. If the batter pivots to bunt, charge. Field the ball with both hands. On sacrifice bunts, you might be able to nail the lead runner at second base with a strong throw. Your catcher will help you make this split-second decision by calling out where to make the throw. If there isn't enough time to cut down the lead runner, throw to the second baseman covering first. Your throw should be on the infield side of first base; this way you'll avoid the mistake of hitting the baserunner in the back.

Don't forget the infielder's Golden Rule: *When in doubt, get the sure out*.

The Cut-off Play

As first baseman, you serve as "cut-off man" on plays to the plate. Therefore, you must learn to anticipate these plays before they happen. (Please note: Some managers divide cut-off duties between the first baseman and third baseman. If that's so, the first baseman is cut-off man on balls hit to center and right field; the third baseman for all balls hit to the left side of the outfield.)

THE CUT-OFF PLAY: Line up directly between the ball and home plate. Listen for the catcher's instructions.

Stand about fifteen feet from the catcher, in a direct line between the outfielder and home plate. Give a good target by holding your hands up above your shoulders. As the ball comes toward you, listen to the catcher. If the throw is strong and on-line, the catcher will probably tell you to let it go. If the throw is weak, or if it's off-line, then he'll tell you to cut the ball off. In this case, you will quickly turn, set, and throw the ball home or relay the ball to second or third. Again, this is a play of instant decisions. Get help from your teammates so you know what to do with the ball *before* you get it.

Points to Remember

- ◆ Learn to anticipate bunts and cut-off plays.
- ◆ Charge all bunts.

- When in doubt, get the sure out.
- Listen for the catcher on cut-off plays.
- On throws to first, toss the ball underhand with a bowler's motion.

DRILL #9—The Scoop Play

A ball thrown in the dirt is the most difficult play for a first baseman to make. Many players simply turn their heads to the sky and blindly swipe at the ball. Needless to say, that's not an effective technique for making the play. The key is to keep your head down and your eye on the ball. Cushion the ball as it hits your glove by pulling it in toward your body. Be sure to use both hands.

Use tennis balls to practice your technique. Position yourself in front of a fence (so you don't have to chase every ball you miss). Have a teammate or friend throw you balls in the dirt. Get into the habit of watching the ball all the way and cushioning the throw with your glove. It's a tough, tough play—you'll need a lot of practice to become good at it. So, what are you waiting for? Start practicing!

Second and Short:
The Keystone Combination

Second base and shortstop are the heart of the defense. In fact, the second baseman and shortstop are commonly called the "keystone combination." A keystone is a term that builders and architects use. It refers to a central stone of an arch that locks the pieces together. Think about it: *A center that locks the pieces together*. That's exactly what you do when you play short or second—you lock the defense together. You plug up the holes to prevent balls from getting through.

The second baseman and shortstop share many duties. Let's begin by looking at plays that are common to each position. Then we'll talk about specifics for each individual position.

Relay Throws

On long hits to the outfield, it's better for a team to make two short throws than try to make one very long throw. That's where you come in. If the ball is hit deep to the outfield, run out about twenty feet towards the ball. Position yourself with your arms raised so the outfielder can find you quickly. To save time, stand sideways, with your throwing shoulder aimed at the outfielder. Catch the ball, then turn your head toward the infield. Take a quick skip-and-step toward your target. Put your whole body into a hard, low throw.

THE RELAY THROW: Speed, teamwork, and accuracy are the keys to this important play.

It's important to listen for instructions on where to throw the ball. A teammate may yell, "Third!" or "Home!" If there's no throw to make, quickly run the ball into the infield. The ball can't do your team any good if it stays in the outfield.

Tag Plays

For tag plays, position yourself behind second base, slightly to the first base side. Bend your knees and back, giving a low target about waist high. Catch the ball and lay your glove down between the base and runner. This way the runner tags himself out! After you make the tag, pull your glove away. You don't want the ball jarred loose by the runner.

THE TAG: Be in position to catch the ball and slap it down between the bag and the oncoming runner. Cover the ball with your bare hand.

Points to Remember

- Second and short are the "keystone combination"—the center that locks the defense together.
- On relay throws, position yourself directly in line with the outfielder and the base to which you'll most likely throw the ball.
- On tag plays, place your glove between the bag and the runner—let the runner tag himself out.

Playing Second Base

Since the second baseman usually makes fairly short throws to either first or second base, you can afford to play fairly deep. By playing back, you'll be able to cover more territory. Position yourself halfway between first and second base, about five feet behind the basepath. Adjust your position according to the game situation. For example, if a lefty batter comes up, move a few steps closer to first. If it's late in a close game and there's a runner on third, it may be appropriate for you to try to cut off the run at the plate. You'll have to edge in, positioning yourself in front of the basepath. Get ready to stop a sharply hit ball and throw home. Again—positioning depends upon the game situation.

A Variety of Throws

Unlike outfielders, a second baseman must make short, quick throws from a variety of angles. At times it's best to throw sidearm; other times you'll need to toss the ball underhand. You should practice all kinds of throws from different areas of the playing field. But don't forget the tried-and-true: *Throw the ball with an overhand motion whenever possible.*

112

> QUICK TIP: On sidearm throws, the ball should be released below your belt and above your knees.

Force Plays at Second

With a runner on first and a ground ball hit to the shortstop or third baseman, there's a good chance the play will come to second. It's your job to cover. Move to the bag quickly, easing in as you near it. Give a chest-high target as you straddle the bag. As the ball comes to you, step with one foot toward the ball. The other foot, of course, must be on the bag. Avoid the runner by stepping toward the infield side of the bag as soon as you catch the ball. Since it's a force play, you don't have to make a tag.

Pop-ups

You should take all pop-ups in your immediate playing area, including those behind the mound. You are also responsible for balls hit behind the first baseman. You have a better angle on the ball, so it's an easier play for you to make. The most difficult play is the shallow pop-up hit into the outfield. As you know, it's easier to catch balls when you are moving in than when you are moving back. That's why, whenever possible, the outfielder is instructed to call for any pop-up he can reach. However, you should keep going for the ball until the outfielder calls for it. Even if you call for it first, the outfielder might call for it second. If that's the case, get out of the way—it's the outfielder's play.

Covering Bunts and Backing Up

You have to cover first base on bunt plays. It can be a long distance to run, so you should anticipate the play before it hap-

THE SECOND BASEMAN MUST COVER first base on all bunt attempts.

pens. On a bunt, the first baseman charges toward home plate. As she does this, you must run over to first. Position yourself with your left foot touching the edge of the bag. This gives the runner a clear line up the basepath—and it gives your teammates a clear view of their target. After you make the catch, quickly step off the bag. Be alert for other baserunners trying to "steal" an extra base.

Back up your teammates whenever you can. You'll be able to do this on grounders to first and on throws to second base with the shortstop covering. Also, with runners on base, be alert for poorly thrown balls from the catcher to the pitcher. It's a live ball; the runners are free to run if the ball gets loose. You may save a run by staying on your toes and anticipating the worst.

Points to Remember

- ◆ Your positioning depends upon the game situation.
- ◆ Throw in an overhand motion whenever possible.
- ◆ Cover or back up second base on force plays.

114

- Go for pop-ups in the outfield, but give way if the outfielder calls you off.
- Cover first base on bunts.

Playing Shortstop

On most teams, the shortstop is the finest, smoothest, slickest fielder. Not only can you cover a wide area, but you have a cannon for an arm. Still, it's not the sensational plays that are most important. You are valuable to your team because of your consistency. Time and again, you make every play look easy. Your smooth footwork, your quiet confidence, and your steady glove make you a key member of the defense.

Positioning

Unless you have a very, very strong arm, it doesn't help to play too deep. Generally, it's best to position yourself about halfway between third and second, slightly behind the basepath. Judge the ability of your third baseman. If he ranges well to the left, you may be able to "cheat" a little toward second base. Adjust your position as each new situation occurs in the game.

The Crossover Step

As shortstop, you have a lot of ground to cover, ranging far to both your right and left. Getting a quick first step is essential. Practice using the crossover step until it becomes second nature to you. The key is to make your first step by "crossing over" with your leg. For complete instructions, see Drill #6 in the chapter, "Playing the Outfield."

THE CROSSOVER
STEP is your key to
covering extra ground
in the infield.

For quick starts, keep your body low to the ground. Don't try
to run with your body fully extended—take quick, short steps.

Force Plays at Second

With a runner at first, there may be a force play at second base,
since it's always best to cut down the lead runner. The second
baseman covers if the ball is hit to you or the third baseman. You

116

cover second if the pitcher, first baseman, catcher, or second baseman fields the ball.

Get to the bag quickly. Give a chest-high target by straddling just behind the bag with both feet. Step toward the ball as it's thrown to you. Be careful—avoid stepping into the basepath; step either to the left or right of the bag. Once you make the catch, get out of the way of the runner.

Pop-ups

Call for all pop-ups in your immediate playing area, including those behind the mound. You are also responsible for balls hit behind the third baseman. It's an easier play for you to make because you have a better angle on the ball. The toughest play is a shallow pop-up into the outfield. If both you and the outfielder can reach the ball, it's the outfielder's ball. Nevertheless, you should try to catch all outfield pop-ups. But

AFTER A FORCE PLAY AT SECOND BASE, a strong overhand throw just might nip the runner at first for a rare double play!

117

listen for the outfielder. If he calls for the ball, let him have it. It's important to avoid dangerous collisions.

Covering Bunts and Backing Up

It's your responsibility to cover second on almost all bunt plays. (The only exception is when there's a runner on second base. In such a situation, the coach may ask you to cover third.)

Let's say there's a runner at first. On a sacrifice bunt, you should quickly run to the bag. If the fielder has a chance to throw the lead runner out at second, call for the ball. Take the throw by keeping one foot on the bag and stepping toward the infield. Once you make the catch, quickly step off the bag toward the pitcher's mound. If there isn't time to nab the lead runner, point to first and yell, "First base!"

Backing up is another key responsibility of the shortstop. You should back up all grounders to third base and pitcher. Also, back up second base whenever the second baseman covers on steal plays. Like the second baseman, you should be alert if the ball gets loose on throws from the catcher to the pitcher. With runners on base, back up each throw.

Points to Remember

- Play on your toes—get a quick first step.
- Use the crossover step whenever you range to the right or left.
- Cover second base on bunt plays, u*nless* there's already a runner on second, in which case you may be asked to cover third.
- Go for all pop-ups to the outfield...*until* you hear the outfielder call for the ball.
- Back up your teammates.

DRILL #10—The Rundown Play

This drill is appropriate for all infielders. You'll need four fielders and one runner to execute this drill.

The rundown is an example of team defense. It is used when a baserunner is trapped between bases. To make this play, you'll need a high level of cooperation, with each player knowing exactly what's expected of him.

A rundown can occur between first and second, second and third, or third and home. In this drill, practice the rundown between first and second. To begin, the first baseman and second baseman should take their positions near their respective bases. A runner should stand on the basepath between the two bases. The catcher should back up first; the shortstop backs up second.

The second baseman holds the ball. He forces the runner toward first by holding the ball in a throwing position and

THE RUNDOWN PLAY: Always hold the ball in your bare hand, ready to throw it to a teammate.

119

sprinting toward the runner. The shortstop stays back to cover second base. As the runner nears first, the second baseman throws to first and then returns to back up the shortstop. If the first baseman can, she tags the runner. If the runner changes direction and heads toward second, the first baseman charges the runner and throws to the shortstop to make the tag. The catcher assumes the position at first; the first baseman retreats and backs up the catcher.

A few tips: 1) Be careful not to hit the runner with the ball. 2) It's best to force the runner back rather than forward. This way, if the runner somehow eludes the tag, he'll only be safe on first base, not second. 3) Don't make too many throws. The more throws, the greater the chance of error. Two or three throws is best.

Playing Third Base

Welcome to third base, otherwise known as the Hot Corner. It's a position for a tough player with lightning reflexes and a thunderous arm. In a flash, a big right-handed batter might rip the ball down the line, making you feel like a goalie in the National Hockey League. Then the next batter might drop a slow bunt down the line. You'll need to charge the ball, field it, and throw on the run without a second to spare. It's a play that demands the agility and grace of a ballet dancer. Sound easy? It isn't. But then again, they don't call it the Hot Corner for nothing!

There is, by the way, an advantage to playing at the Hot Corner. Because ground balls get to you so fast, you often have time to knock the ball down, recover, get set, and throw in time to get the runner.

Positioning

The third baseman should play a few feet behind the bag, fairly close to the line. If a lefty batter is at the plate, you should move in even with the bag and towards second base.

As you position yourself, you have several things to think about. First, you've got to protect the line. A grounder that gets past you down the third base line will probably go for a double or a triple. So don't leave too much of a hole to your right. A good third baseman can range well to the left. Go for every ball that's hit to your left side—even if it means cutting in front of the shortstop. It's an easier throw for you to make than the shortstop, because you are moving towards first, while the shortstop's momentum takes him away from first.

QUICK TIP: Be prepared to dive for balls going down the line. You may only knock the ball down, but you'll keep the hit from becoming a double or triple.

Fielding Bunts and Slow Rollers

You must always be aware of the possibility of a bunt or a slow roller. That's why you can't sit back on your heels and wait for a hot smash to come your way.

If a player does bunt or hit a slow roller, charge the ball quickly. Keep your body low to the ground, with your glove leading the charge. Set and field the ball with both hands. Quickly bring the ball out of your glove and back to throwing position. Take a quick skip and fire overhand to first.

As you improve on this play, you may want to practice throwing on the run. It's all in the footwork. Field the ball as you step forward with your right foot. Quickly bring both hands up to your belt as you take the next step with your left foot. Extend your arm into throwing position. Complete your throw as your right foot comes forward once more. But remember, you shouldn't panic or try to throw when you are off-balance. It will only lead to unnecessary errors.

Pop-ups

You should handle all infield pop-ups on the third base side of the diamond. You should also handle foul balls. But, like the first baseman, it is best to let others take charge of pop-ups that are hit over your head. Often these are easier plays for the left fielder or shortstop to make. This doesn't mean don't try to catch the ball. Try to make the play—but be alert for someone to call you off the ball.

The Tag

The tag at third base is relatively easy...if you go about things the right way. For a throw from the catcher, for example, position yourself *behind* the bag. In this position, you should be able to catch the ball and slap down the tag in one, smooth motion. Let the runner slide into your glove. Got 'em!

Team Play

Be alert to back up balls that are thrown to second base from right field. If the ball gets past, it's your job to stop it. However, you must also be careful not to leave third base unattended. Work out a system of backing up with the pitcher. Sometimes it makes more sense for the pitcher to back up plays at second.

At times, you may field a grounder with a runner at first. In this case, look to make your play at second base. Give the second baseman a strong overhand throw about chest high.

Points to Remember

◆ If you knock the ball down, recover quickly. You may still have time to throw the runner out.

- Observe your opponents—try to anticipate bunts.
- Field any grounders to your left that you can get to, even if it means cutting in front of the shortstop. You have a much easier throw.
- Charge all bunts and slow rollers; it's important to get a quick start.

LAST WORD: BALANCE, BABY, BALANCE

The theme of balance has come up often in this book because balance is so important to your game. When you hit, when you throw, when you field—throughout the game you must always be balanced. Balance gives you a stable base to move right or left, forward or back. Balance helps keep your body under control. The same applies to emotional balance. You can't get too mad, or too sad, or too wrapped up in the game. Sometimes you win; sometimes you lose. Either way, it's not the end of the world (despite the way some grownups might act). To play well—and for that matter, to live well—you must have balance.

That's my last word—now go out and play ball!

ABOUT THE AUTHOR

James Preller began his Little League playing career as a scrappy southpaw with good control, soft hands, and average power. Preller had his best year at age ten, while playing for the Cardinals of the Wantagh Little League on Long Island, New York. That year he pitched, played first base, and even got a hit once in a while. His "career year" was curtailed when he fractured an index finger while attempting to bunt. Though Preller went on to play baseball for years to come, nothing ever quite matched his 1971 season for enthusiasm, excitement, and great times. For him it was pure Little League—baseball like it ought to be.

Mr. Preller is a freelance writer residing in Albany, New York. This is his fifth book for children.

NOTES

NOTES

NOTES